The Jungian Experience

Marie-Louise von Franz, Honorary Patron

**Studies in Jungian Psychology
by Jungian Analysts**

Daryl Sharp, General Editor

The Jungian Experience

Analysis and Individuation

James A. Hall, M.D.

With gratitude to those who have taught me what I know: my analysts and my analysands.

Canadian Cataloguing in Publication Data

Hall, James Albert, 1934-
  The Jungian experience

(Studies in Jungian psychology by Jungian analysts; 26)

Includes bibliographical references and index.

ISBN 0-919123-25-2

1. Jung, C.G. (Carl Gustav), 1875-1961.
2. Psychoanalysis.   3. Individuation.   I. Title.
II. Series.

BF109.J8H35 1986   150.19'54   C86-094509-X

INNER CITY BOOKS
Box 1271, Station Q, Toronto, Canada M4T 2P4
Telephone (416) 927-0355

Honorary Patron: Marie-Louise von Franz.
Publisher and General Editor: Daryl Sharp.
Editorial Board: Fraser Boa, Daryl Sharp, Marion Woodman.
Executive Assistants: Vicki Cowan, Ben Sharp.

INNER CITY BOOKS was founded in 1980 to promote the understanding and practical application of the work of C.G. Jung.

Cover: Elephant & Castle, by Jessie Kate Cowan-Sharp (1983).

Index by Daryl Sharp

Printed and bound in Canada by Webcom Limited

Contents

See final pages for descriptions of other Inner City Books

Recognize what is before your eyes,
and what is hidden will be revealed to you.
—The Gospel of Thomas.

C.G. Jung
1875-1961

(Jung at the age of 83; photo by Karsh of Ottawa)

Introduction

A Personal Statement

All psychological statements are personal. One cannot speak a psychological truth without simultaneously making a confession. We see what we are permitted to see by our personal vision, which is always to some degree uniquely our own. And yet, in the experience of life (or in life accelerated by analysis) we find over and over again that what we have considered to be our own unique and personal understanding and pain is actually universal, the shared experience of mankind. We can lose our individuality outside in the swells and currents of collective life, but we can also abandon ourselves to the unconscious within, naively accepting as our own personal psyche whatever voices are thrown up from the underside of the mind.

In the midst of this dilemma between the inner and outer worlds, either of which may consume us if we are unaware, there occurs the delicate but basic process of individuation. The small, statistically insignificant, individual human psyche is the only carrier for all the sound and fury of the outer world as well as the only outlet in consciousness for the vast inner world of the archetypes, the distilled human experience of our life on this planet.

C.G. Jung's view of the human situation appreciates this unique and valuable position of the individual human being. In one of his intuitive visions, Jung felt that the dead await eagerly the news of any human being, even the most insignificant person in the world, for it is only in the difficult world of human life that decisions and insights can be gained.[1] Perhaps the dead exist in a timeless archetypal world where it is not possible to learn new truths because of a lack of separation of events in time and space. In this intuition, Jung is close to the Buddhist view that it is better to be born into the human world than into the world of the gods, for the gods are so powerful and live for such an incredibly long time that it is hard for them to realize what is most readily learned in human life: the transient nature of all created things.

Jung's insights cover a period from the close scientific observations of the word-association experiment, with which he began his

9

career, to the mature and mystical speculations of his later years, reflected in his autobiography in chapters on such topics as life after physical death. The broad canvas of Jungian thought spans clinical concerns of treatment, personal religious development and scientific questions about the nature of matter, mind and causality. It is too complex to be entirely contained within the area of clinical treatment. The experience of the Jungian model of the psyche involves analysis in the usual clinical sense *plus* life experience *and* religious and philosophical reflection upon that experience. Hence the subtitle of this book is *analysis and individuation.* Neither analysis alone, nor individuation without the reflective aspects of conscious work on oneself, constitutes the Jungian experience.

This broad canvas of Jungian theory first attracted me to the study of Jungian psychology, and the attraction has never dimmed. I have found the insights of others to be of great value, but it has always been possible to find a place for them in the Jungian framework. The reverse, however, has never been possible: I could not fit the range and depth of Jungian thought into a more restricted container.

I became a Jungian analyst in a meandering way. First I had wanted to be an architect, inspired by experiences with my father's building business in eastern Texas. But emotional tensions led me toward medicine, for I felt that in medicine it might be possible to reconcile my strong religious feelings with the apparent inevitability of entering military service during wartime. After a year of premedical studies, I again changed course, enrolling in the College of Arts and Sciences at the University of Texas in Austin. Most of my undergraduate studies were related to writing and I graduated without a major field. A year in graduate English (actually studying journalism and editing the *Ranger,* the college humor magazine), led me toward considering a doctorate in English and a career in teaching. Those plans ended in a period of depression, during which the whole direction of my life seemed uncertain. In retrospect, it was the flight of the *puer aeternus* (the eternal adolescent) when faced with the realities of an actual world.[2]

I returned to premedical studies and a year later entered Southwestern Medical School, a branch of the University of Texas. There followed years of completing medical training and internship, three years of psychiatry residence at Duke and Southwestern, followed by a brief thirteen months in practice before I was drafted, as a physician, during the Vietnam war.

Two years in the Army forced me to develop assertive parts of my personality that had lain dormant in the shadow of the puer. It also gave time for study, more family time, and permitted me to pass psychiatry boards.

A strange experience the night before my psychiatry board exam convinced me of the reality of the unconscious and the importance of dreams. Although I do not remember a dream that night, I am certain that it was an unremembered dream that restored my psychic equilibrium just before the examinations. I had been studying for six months, often with other psychiatrists and with one of the neurologists stationed at Ft. Gordon. The neurologist and myself drove together from Augusta, Georgia, to New York City, reviewing notes along the way. The night before the exam, we had dinner at a Chinese restaurant across the street from our hotel. I remember that he had squid in its own ink—and the blackness of that dish could not have been darker than my mood. I felt totally inadequate, in spite of great preparation, and was convinced that I would fail the examinations. My last thoughts before going to sleep near midnight were what I might say when I returned to Augusta as a failure.

When I awoke, even before opening my eyes, I was aware of a complete shift in my mental state. Not only did I have no anxiety, but there seemed to be a sense of confidence and certainty that everything would be fine. I opened my eyes and looked at my watch. It was a little after two in the morning. I remembered no dream, but felt as if I had dreamed something profound. It was easy to return to a restful sleep and I awoke in the same confident mood.

The board examinations went smoothly, and I can even say they were a pleasurable experience. I realized that what had happened in the middle of the night was an example of what Jung called *enantiodromia,* a term he borrowed from the Greek philosopher Heraclitus. Enantiodromia is the principle that opposites, at their extremes, tend to turn into one another.[3]

One of the most graphic representations of the principle of enantiodromia is the Taoist symbol of the *yang* (masculine) and *yin* (feminine) forces combined in a symbol of totality, the *t'ai chi tu,* represented as two "fishes"—a black one with a white "eye" and a white one with a black "eye." In later years, I came to a deep appreciation of the concept of enantiodromia, which is involved in the psychological unification of opposites. The tension between opposites in the individual human psyche is part of the basic nature of the mind, but played out unconsciously, particularly with projections onto other persons of one's opposite or shadow characteristics, it can lead to great human misery. When the tension of opposites is constellated in large political groups, or between nations, it can lead to unbelievable suffering and disorder.

Through personal experiences such as these, the theoretical model of Jungian analysis was fleshed out with depth and meaning. Although the reading of Jolande Jacobi's *Complex/Archetype/Symbol* had excited me, my subsequent reading of Jung had in some ways been confusing. I could become excited about the deep implications of his writing, but was unable to make the bridge to my everyday world of clinical and personal experience. At one time this became such a problem that I was unable to read more than a few pages of Jung's writing without bogging down in the gap between its profound meaning and the everyday world.

Once again, the unconscious itself gave me a way through the dilemma. Just before I entered the army medical service, I had a spontaneous vision of Jung as a rocket ship that had been propelled high into space by the expulsion of a vast amount of material— which was simultaneously all the books he had written and, to be blunt, plain shit. This was both a freeing and a disturbing vision, particularly since I knew that I must discuss it at once with my Jungian analyst, Rivkah Kluger, who had worked very closely with Jung himself. I was afraid she would reject me or consider that the vision simply showed my resistance to Jungian thought. However, she interpreted it in the same manner that I did: Jung's writings were for Jung himself a means of propulsion in his own remarkable journey of personal individuation. But seen from another vantage point, they were only excrement, of no value.

But excrement, shit, has another meaning in alchemy, the esoteric forerunner to modern chemistry (which Jung was led to study by a series of dreams, thereby discovering the historical precursor of his analytical psychology). The most valuable alchemical substance was the Philosophers' Stone, sometimes called the elixir of life. It had the remarkable capacity to transform base metals into gold or to heal any illness (although if taken with the wrong attitude it could also be a deadly poison). In psychological terms, the

Philosophers' Stone, or *lapis,* would be the archetypal Self, the regulating center of the psyche. If the ego can truly contact the Self, it is at once a healing experience for the ego, but also a defeat, since the ego then realizes that it is only a part of the psyche, not its actual center. Experience of the Self is a sobering antidote for psychic inflation.[4]

And with what material did the alchemist start in order to try to produce the *lapis,* the thing of highest value? One of the metaphorical descriptions of the beginning material, the *prima materia,* is excrement or shit! This *prima materia* is found everywhere, is despised or considered of no value, worthless—sometimes called "the orphan," belonging to no person or family, unconnected to the everyday world of social values. In psychological language, the *prima materia* is one's ordinary, everyday life experience. In the neurotic person considering Jungian analysis, the ups and downs of everyday life are often scorned, although that is precisely the material through which, with the proper psychological work, one can approach the *lapis,* the Self, the experience of very highest value.

My vision suggested, then, that Jung's writings were a rich source of this *prima materia,* from which one might find ways toward the Self. But his *Collected Works* contained no ready-made panacea; they were the place to begin. This vision thus corrected my puer tendency to seek a father figure whose insights would provide all the answers, and at the same time it set me squarely upon the necessary path of working with my own *prima materia* toward my own potential experience of the *lapis.*

While working with the same Jungian analyst, I had another dream that put Jung's work into perspective. In this dream my analyst was cooking in her kitchen, while I and one of Jung's grandsons (whom I had met when he was working in Dallas) were waiting to sample the meal. On the counter between the kitchen and the room in which we stood was a case of some half dozen steak knives (which reminded me of a case my own father owned). Suddenly one of the knives cracked with a loud sound of breaking metal! As I went to pick up the cracked knife, it suddenly turned into "Jung's sword," which was so large that by standing on tip-toe I could barely keep the point of it from touching the floor. Just below the hilt where I was holding it, a piece of metal was missing from the blade. Jung's grandson remarked, "It's a shame that the official guardians won't let us repair it!"

My association to the cracking knife was to one of Jung's own experiences, where a bread knife cracked inside a drawer.[5] It was one of the parapsychological events that led Jung to the concept of *synchronicity,* the strange parallel in meaning between an inner subjective event and an outer objective event, discussed below in chapter 9. Because the dream paralleled this important experience of Jung's, I took it to mean that I indeed had a true connection to the soul and spirit of Jung's work.

I worried for years, however, about the phrase, "It's a shame that the official guardians won't let us repair it!" Only within the last two years have I felt a sense of what that might actually mean. The one defect in Jungian psychology as it is often presented is that a too symbolic approach may be taken! If too much emphasis is placed upon the symbolic mode of understanding, the real goal of Jungian analysis can be missed—the goal of the *lapis,* which is *within* the world and yet is capable of transforming the world.

This too symbolic approach to Jungian analysis has become evident in at least one school of Jungian thought, that called "archetypal psychology." In that approach, the ego is slighted, the Self considered "monotheistic," and emphasis is placed upon "deepening" experience away from the "dayworld" of consciousness into the "underworld" of symbolic archetypal forms.[6] To me that is an unfortunate deviation from the direction of Jung's work. Jung himself always emphasized that the ego is an indispensable part of the individuation process; the ego must not only experience the unconscious, but must take an attitude toward it. Without the ego, the unconscious is helpless to actualize itself effectively in the world, which is the essence of the individuation process.

One of the reasons for writing this book, therefore, is to guide the person seeking Jungian analysis toward the classical tradition of analysis, where individuation is clearly the goal. Jung's vision is so vast that it will be decades before its full implications will be understood. Edward Edinger may well be right when he calls Jung the *epochal man* of the next phase of human history, the harbinger and example of a new way of living.[7] This book is meant to correct some common misconceptions and to give the person considering Jungian analysis a head start that will enhance the actual experience. As well, the reader may gain a basic idea of what is to be accomplished in analysis.

Work on the shadow, that "dark" alter ego that in some ways is the equivalent of Freud's concept of the "id," constitutes much of the ordinary work of psychotherapy and analysis. Although the shadow seems unacceptable to one's present ego-image, it often contains unrecognized positive qualities that are needed for further individuation. One of my friends in Zurich, when studying with me for the propaedeuticum examination (the theory examination at the midpoint of training) remarked wistfully that he originally had gone into Jungian analysis because he had heard that the unconscious was a treasure trove of jewels. Pounding the table, he exclaimed, "And I *want* my treasure trove of jewels!"—adding that he still had to deal with shadow problems and the residual complexes of childhood trauma.

Another analyst told of jumping over the fence at the ruins of Epidaurus in Greece, the ancient healing shrine of Asclepius, the Greek god of medicine, and "incubating" (the classical expression for sleeping in the sacred Thalmos chamber of the temple) in order to get a healing dream. All he got, he said with disgust, were more shadow dreams.

Many years later, an analysand of my own dreamed that he indeed owned a treasure chest of jewels in the basement of his house, but realized in the dream that although he could go to the cellar to view them, he was not allowed to bring them into the dayworld of everyday life: they were a great treasure, but had no "cash value." Bridging the gap between the potential treasures of the archetypal world and the world of ego-consciousness is one way of characterizing the process of individuation, actualizing (to the extent possible in empirical life) the unique individual potentialities of one's own psyche.

In addition to those readers considering entering Jungian analysis, this volume is intended to help therapists of other theoretical backgrounds to better understand the clinical application of the classical Jungian approach. Many of the principles can be used in an eclectic practice of psychotherapy, even without formal Jungian training. Toward that end, I have made a particular effort to illustrate the theoretical points with clear clinical examples. The weaving together of theory and practice is essential to avoid the pitfall of excessive symbolism that the Jungian approach invites.

In its application, Jungian theory actually offers one of the most practical and down-to-earth approaches to the human psyche in the entire field of psychotherapeutic thought, but Jungian literature generally does not clearly demonstrate how to translate the concepts into practice. While it is admittedly difficult to do this without the experience of a personal analysis, it is still possible to absorb the true spirit of Jung's work through written material of a more clinically descriptive nature. Many of the titles in this series by Inner City Books, and the recently inaugurated Jungian journal *Chiron,* have this aim. A book with similar intent, though written from the standpoint of humanistic psychology, is *Fully Alive,* which features a number of practical exercises.[8]

A third group of readers who may find this book of value are those already engaged in Jungian analysis, either as analysands or as Jungian analysts. In its original conception, this volume was to be a discussion of psychopathology from a Jungian point of view, a corrective to the strong emphasis on syndrome diagnoses in the current practice of the American Psychiatric Association (as presented in Diagnostic and Statistical Manual III, which itself is slated for revision in the next few years). There is still need for such discussion, but it must await clarification of some of the various trends within analytical psychology itself, as outlined by Andrew Samuels in *Jung and the Post-Jungians.*[9]

Finally, I sincerely hope this book brings the Jungian experience, both analysis and individuation, closer for the many who seek it. In their future lives and experience the spirit and soul of Jungian psychology may truly exist in the world.

1

The Troubled Person

Why do people seek psychotherapy or analysis? Many reasons may be given, but there is usually one underlying motivation: the sense that all is not right with one's life, that somehow a deeper meaning or purpose has been missed. In many instances this is associated with a sense of guilt, as if oneself were somehow responsible for the difficulty. Often the presenting symptoms are abortive attempts to find the right path—a series of broken marriages or relationships, a recurrent pattern of difficulty with work or family, or simply an overwhelming sense that something is not right in life, that it is lacking in depth and significant goals.

In spite of seeking psychotherapy because of a deep sense of personal discomfort, the troubled person usually hopes that somehow it is not at all his or her own basic problem, that the real problem is the family, the marriage partner or the circumstances of life. There is a deep-seated human desire not to be at fault, not to be the one who must change. Although the troubled person comes to the psychotherapist or analyst asking for help in changing, there is often this unspoken desire to be approved just as one is, and that the burden of change will be placed on someone else's shoulders.

An example that will always remain in my memory occurred years ago, in the early days of my analytic practice. The young woman had been my patient for several months, working on neurotic problems of depression, when she said during one weekly session, "I don't have much money and these sessions are terribly expensive for me; since you know what's wrong with me and I don't, why don't you just tell me, so I can work on it faster and save money?"

I felt sorry for her and made the mistake of taking her request at its conscious value, without remembering the unconscious meanings that attached to it as well. I told her as concisely as I could what I saw about her behavior and attitudes that were making her unhappy.

With an angry gesture she banged her purse on my desk, exclaiming, "If *that's* the way you feel about me, I'm leaving!"—and she left! I did not see her again for some three months. When she came back, she apologized to me (and I to her) and we resumed useful psychotherapy which led to some real improvement in her condition.

Since then, I have come to a deeper appreciation of the problems of transference and countertransference (discussed in chapter 4), for it is not simply the conscious relationship between the analyst and the analysand that is involved in the analytic constellation. There is also the conscious relation of each party to his or her own unconscious mind, as well as to the unconscious mind of the other person, plus the direct relationship between the unconscious minds of the two persons. Jung called even that a simplified model of the interaction![10]

Although the troubled person comes to the analyst with the barely conscious hope that there will be no need for psychotherapy, yet another part of the personality always recognizes that some vital change is needed. In the initial interview, or series of interviews, this need should become clearer in the mind of both the analyst and the analysand, even if a more definitive formulation must await a trial period of analysis. In fact, the precise formulation of a diagnosis is not often possible (or even desirable except as a gross orienting device). The diagnostic categories currently used in psychiatry are discussed below in chapter 3, but they are designed largely for the collection of data on types of psychiatric problems, without theoretical bias. They are not subtle enough for the conceptualization of the personal struggles within the psyche that are the actual growing points of the individuation process. Nevertheless, the analytic pair of patient and analyst must have some sense of the direction in which they are trying to move, and a general formulation of the problem is helpful, even if it is later revised.

Diagnoses are not without their dangers and side-effects. Patients with a particularly logical frame of mind may go from learning the name of their diagnosis to reading about it in the psychiatric literature, often becoming frightened that everything said in the theoretical description of the diagnosis will necessarily happen to them personally. To want to know too strongly what is wrong with oneself is often counterproductive and may lead more to fearful fantasy than to deeper understanding.

When I myself first entered psychiatric training, I often suffered from finding something about myself in the theoretical description of virtually every psychiatric disorder in the textbook. It was only with accumulating clinical experience that I was able to see these theoretical descriptions in perspective. Without clinical experience, the descriptions convey too much, particularly to the troubled person who is already strongly convinced that something is amiss, and by coming for consultation has demonstrated a strong motivation to understand what is wrong. The courage is admirable, even necessary, but needs to be applied to understanding the finer meaning of the personal material—often dreams and their associations—rather than to the too-gross descriptions of diagnostic categories.

One of the reasons that everyone has for feeling that there is something wrong inside is the presence in each one of us of what Jung called the *shadow*. The shadow is one of the structural concepts of analytical psychology (discussed more fully here in appendix 1). The term shadow does not imply something evil, but simply refers to what is thrown into the "shade" by that which stands in the "light" of consciousness. When something is approaching consciousness from the unconscious, it comes into a field of evaluation that might be called a field of moral choice. Part of what is approaching may be acceptable and incorporated into the ego, with the unacceptable part being dissociated or repressed into the shadow.

Contents that are acceptable to the person's *ego*—that part of us that is "I" and feels itself to be the center of consciousness—are often incorporated with little difficulty into the *persona,* particularly if they are also acceptable to the cultural situation in which one exists. The persona consists of a "mask," not just in the sense of hiding something, but also in the sense of revealing something—a social or cultural role, for example, as was indicated by the large masks of classical Greek drama. When it "fits well," it enhances and communicates more effectively the true nature of the ego "behind" it; but if it is overused in place of developing an adequate ego, or if it is used to hide the true nature of the ego, pathological states may occur. Too little development of the persona exposes the ego to trauma in a manner analogous to the body having defective coverings of skin.

When the troubled person first comes to the analyst, there is always an element of *persona anxiety* as well as *shadow anxiety*. These two forms of anxiety are perfectly normal, but either may become pathological if it occurs to an extreme degree—either too much anxiety (the usual neurotic pattern) or even too little anxiety, which at its worst indicates psychopathy (inadequate moral development and little concern for the effect of one's actions on others).

In analysis, persona anxiety appears as a fear of revealing to the analyst the actual details of one's life, often the very details that are necessary for a correct understanding of the problem and the proper formulation of a tentative treatment plan. The patient may actually forget the details, and so not report them. More often, however, the material exists in memory but is not volunteered in the analytic dialogue. This is another form of the neurotic defensive hope that what one is truly concerned about in oneself is not crucial and does not have to be analyzed.

Some therapists simply begin without much background data, acquiring it in the course of the analysis; but this does not seem to me the most desirable approach. In the initial sessions, when analyst and analysand are still getting to know each other, questions of work history, family, etc., are analogous to the taking of a personal medical history, that is, they are more neutral in emotional tone. After a transference-countertransference relationship is established, however, the same questions may carry deep unconscious overtones and be responded to more defensively.

If one bit of advice could be taken seriously by every person entering analysis it would save much heartache and even actual dollar expense: *tell the analyst precisely why you feel something is amiss with you.* It is better to tell too much, to overemphasize what is thought to be wrong, than to omit a detail that may be of value. Any analyst who has been long in practice has heard many times all the likely human foibles that the troubled person is hesitant to mention. Although it is difficult to realize, the fear of rejection that the patient is experiencing in withholding shadow material from the analysis is actually the patient's own internal self-rejection, often connected to the core of the neurotic problem. It is also important to understand that *what the patient considers to be the reason for coming to analysis may not be the real underlying reason.*

A number of years ago, a patient in group psychotherapy hesitated for months to tell the group his terrible secret. Finally, with much support and encouragement, he closed his eyes, clenched his fists and shouted, "I'm a faggot!" After several minutes of silence, he opened his eyes, startled that no one had responded emotionally to his frightened confession. Everyone else in the group had realized months before that he was a homosexual, and they still had accepted him. His confession served only his own overstrict conscience, which was part of the psychodynamic structure of his homosexual behavior. As it turned out, he seemed content to maintain his unconscious self-rejection, for he passed up the opportunity to work through the problem. (Perhaps he even helped to maintain rejection—he moved away without paying his large accumulated bill!)

Group therapy is still controversial in Jungian circles. A few analysts, including myself, find it of great value, although Jung felt that group therapy was no substitute for individual analysis.[11] Jung apparently never actually experienced a process-type therapy group, basing his position upon group dynamics in such unstructured social groups as the Psychology Club in Zurich—where persons acted, as Jung observed, with less consciousness than they did as individuals. Group psychotherapy and other variations on the classical Jungian approach are discussed at length in chapter 7.

Persona anxiety is more easily yielded than shadow anxiety, although in practice they are inseparably linked. The anxiety of letting down the persona shield is directly linked to a fear that the shadow may be seen and the person rejected. While the persona is largely within the control of the ego, which generally knows it is there (with the exception of the state of identification with the persona), the quality of the shadow is unknown to the ego. The ego is conscious of part of the shadow, but always feels emotionally that there is more unacceptable material in the shadow than often is found when the shadow actually is revealed.

This shadow anxiety arises to some extent from the manner in which the shadow is formed as a structural part of the personality during early childhood (partly, perhaps, as early as 6-8 months of age). At the time when the ego is being consolidated, it must deal with very primitive judgments of what is accepted by the environment as good (worthy of ego and persona) and what is judged as nonacceptable, with the latter often being repressed or dissociated into the shadow. The shadow is essentially an alternative ego-identity, containing contents that could have been incorporated into the ego if it had developed in a different environment.

A common example in virtually every "civilized" society is the repression into the shadow of even normal ranges of anger. Although such assertiveness may be necessary for the balanced growth of the personality, the fact that it is dissociated into the shadow at an early age means that any return of this repressed material will evoke in the ego the sense that something of dangerous proportions is being reawakened. Much of ordinary psychotherapy, as well as the early stages of Jungian analysis, focuses on becoming aware of this shadow material and reworking it in the light of the judgment of a more developed ego. Although the shadow feels dangerous to the ego, it may actually contain qualities that are needed for the person's further individuation.

For the persona mask to be dropped and the shadow examined, the analysand must feel that the process occurs within a safe container, safer than the ordinary world that the persona was meant to keep at an appropriately safe distance—to allow for a personal world of subjective choice and privacy. This safe boundary of the analytical container is a vital part of the analytical relationship, and is discussed in chapter 4.

The Jungian Vision

Assuming that the troubled person seeks psychotherapy because of a deep intuitive sense that something is wrong, that an inner change is necessary, why specifically seek Jungian analysis?

Many do so because they have read some of Jung's work, or have had a positive response to his approach. Often they are attracted to the theoretical view of the unconscious as a creative matrix of all conscious life, not simply a repository of what has been repressed. Many people instinctively feel this to be the true state of things, just as there is a widespread consensus that dreams are meaningful (as discussed below in chapter 6). The Jungian vision is of a coherent and meaningful psychic whole existing in a world in which there are processes of growth to be facilitated and processes of breakdown that must be responsibly handled. It is a vision of a world in which the individual psyche matters.

Like everything else, however, the Jungian vision can be misused. Some troubled persons seek Jungian analysis in the mistaken belief that they can deal with the large archetypal issues and ignore their own personal psychology. They may actively avoid dealing with painful personal material from the past. This is not consistent with the classical Jungian tradition, for Jung himself never repudiated the usefulness of *reductive analysis*, his term for the type of psychotherapy that Freud advocated in which current problems were "reduced" to the effects of past events still active in the unconscious.

In the ideal situation, the Jungian analyst would be able to engage the troubled person in a reductive analysis, if that is indicated, or in what Jung called the *synthetic* mode, one of symbolic understanding and synthesis of conflicting elements in the service of the individuation process, should that seem more appropriate. If a current conflict actually arises from psychological complexes closely patterned upon past events, the reductive approach may be an efficient procedure to employ. In the next chapter, the theory of complexes will be discussed; it offers a way of reconciling the apparent incompatibility of reductive and synthetic modes of analysis.

Analysis: Frequency and Duration

Persons seeking analysis are frequently and justifiably concerned about the amount of time and expense that may be involved. It is generally assumed that analysis requires years of work, often several sessions weekly, as in the traditional Freudian model, whereas Jungian analysis, and other forms of psychotherapy, are often seen as more rapid or efficient alternatives. Much of the controversy surrounding analysis arises from a difficulty of defining the analytic process in terms of stages and results, so that people tend to fall back upon defining it in terms of technique—number of hours per week, whether one sits face to face with the analyst or reclines on a couch, etc.

The fact is that Jungian analysts are by no means of a uniform mind on these matters. Although most Jungian analysis is done face to face, some Jungians (particularly those trained in England in the Society for Analytical Psychology) frequently use the couch and several appointments per week. In the United States, the most usual arrangement is for analyst and patient to sit facing each other, meeting no more than once or twice weekly. Some Jungians use techniques other than those of classical analysis, including group psychotherapy, projective techniques such as sandtray constructions, art therapy, hypnotherapy, marital therapy, etc. Some do a limited amount of consultation by telephone, but usually only with analysands who have worked for some time in personal face-to-face analysis.

The frequency of analytic sessions can vary from analyst to

analyst and with the severity of the problem. The length of time that one is likely to be in formal analysis is difficult to determine. It is far easier to determine when a troubled person should enter analysis than to say when it is to be terminated. (This problem is specifically addressed in chapter 5.) Trying to estimate how long one will be in analysis is like asking how long it will take one to learn a foreign language, master a musical instrument or build a house. There are many factors: the intensity and frequency of work, innate skill, the availability of the necessary materials and so on.

As a practical matter, it is best to judge one's progress in Jungian analysis only about every six months. To try to evaluate changes at more frequent intervals often leads to overemphasis on brief fluctuations that may not as yet be consolidated in a stable form in the personality. Although many persons may remain in Jungian analysis for years, it is unusual for them to be working on the same problems for which they originally came into analysis. The process that one enters in Jungian analysis is at heart the process of life itself. It therefore has no natural termination other than death, and even then we have no clear vision as to what, if anything, lies beyond. Formal analytical sessions may end or be interrupted at various stages, but the underlying process of individuation, the true meaning of Jungian analysis, is interminable.

One woman who came to me during the first six months of my practice is still in treatment, although there have been times when she has left for extended periods. She is by no means working on the same depression that brought her to analysis; the emphasis now is on personality growth and the movement of her life. Even the parents who were originally such a difficulty for her have reached a stage in life where they are as dependent upon her as she had been upon them.

If there is a choice between an intense period of analytic work and a less intense longer period of work (perhaps because of limited financial resources), it is usually best to choose the longer, but less intense option (except in crisis situations, of course). A more extended analysis allows for a number of life events, which are as crucial as the analysis itself, to take place within the time that the person is in analysis. Again, the Jungian experience is twofold—analysis *and* individuation. Analysis may be scheduled, while the crucial events of individuation cannot be ordered by the ego of either the analyst or the person in analysis.

Jungian Analysts: Training and Background

Virtually all officially-trained Jungian analysts are members of the International Association for Analytical Psychology, the primary certifying body for Jungians, through their membership in the various component societies of the IAAP.

As yet there is no official Jungian "umbrella" organization in North America, although several of the American Jungian professional societies have ratified membership in the Council of American Societies of Jungian Analysts, the embryo of a national organization. The strongly individual emphasis of Jungians, both in theory and practice, has slowed the development of a national group that could certify, as does the IAAP at present, the basic competency of a Jungian analyst, as well as deal more effectively with problems that are peculiar to the analyst practicing in America.

In the absence of a national organization, the person seeking a Jungian analyst can contact one of the American societies that are component members of the IAAP. At the time of writing, there are such societies, each with its own independent training program, in New York, Boston, Chicago, Los Angeles, San Francisco and San Diego. In addition, the Inter-Regional Society of Jungian Analysts, which also does training, has many members throughout the United States and Canada. The addresses of these societies, together with other information on how and where to find Jungian analysts, are given in appendix 2.

In most of the training centers, the profession of Jungian analyst is viewed as a "second career"; that is, one of the qualifications for entering training is evidence that one has already been responsibly engaged in life activities. Training involves personal analysis—usually lasting at least five years and with more than one analyst—and a thorough grounding in the basic principles of analytical psychology, as well as a broad range of academic studies in other disciplines such as mythology and religion.

Jungian analysts vary widely in their clinical training. Some are medical doctors, psychiatrists, psychologists or social workers; others hold various ministerial degrees (and are usually certified by the American Association of Pastoral Counselors). Some Jungian analysts have had no formal clinical background prior to their Jungian training. The Zurich Institute, for instance, is chartered primarily as an educational institution and accepts suitable candidates who have a master's degree in any field (not necessarily clinical), but it considers that graduate analysts have the personal responsibility to meet the legal standards required where they practice. The Zurich training does include courses in psychopathology and requires supervised clinical work.

This diversity of training and background among Jungian analysts adds color and richness to the entire field. The person seeking analysis should inquire into the medical credentials of the analyst, if that is considered of importance. No matter what school of psychoanalytic thought they follow, psychiatrists are trained as physicians, and can therefore prescribe medication for anxiety, depression or more serious mental disturbances. Psychiatrists and some psychologists have access to hospitalization that is sometimes, though rarely, needed. Insurance payments may be available for analysis with some types of practitioners and not with others. These are merely practical considerations and do not reflect upon the quality of any particular school or individual.

The Personal Equation

More important than the analyst's professional training is the *personal equation*, the basic sense of "fit," between analyst and analysand. When one is initially contemplating going into analysis and there is more than one analyst available, it is quite permissible to "shop around." A preliminary interview (for which one will usually pay a fee) is the only way to get a "feel" for what is possible between two persons.

Even the best-trained analyst cannot satisfactorily treat everyone. During psychiatry residency training, I asked one of my professors what he did with patients he really didn't like. He said, "I send them to another psychiatrist I really don't like," adding, "and they always seem to work well together!" My professor was using his own emotional reaction to people in a sensitive way, not faulting either the patient or the other psychiatrist because he did not personally care for them.

Jung clearly believed in the basic importance of what I have called the personal equation between analyst and analysand. He stated that the right tools in the hands of the wrong person will not work, while the wrong tools in the hands of the right person *will* work.[12]

If analysis is not going well, this should be openly and clearly discussed. Frequently that is all that is necessary for the blockages to be removed. Either the analyst or the analysand may introduce the topic. If frank discussion and further analysis do not resolve the impasse, either the analyst or the patient may ask for a consultation with another analyst, which sometimes gives sufficient perspective on the difficulty for the original analysis to resume. If analyst and analysand agree that the analysis does not "move," it may be useful for the analyst to suggest several colleagues that he feels would work well with that particular analysand.

Summary

1. The troubled person who seeks Jungian analysis may come because of a general sense of uneasiness about his or her life, without any clear formulation of the underlying difficulty.

2. The initial visits with the analyst may clarify the presenting problem, although in some cases that will become clear only during the course of analytical work.

3. It is difficult to initially predict the duration of analysis. In general, a longer analysis with less frequency is preferable to a shorter, more intense analysis because the Jungian experience involves both analysis and individuation, which includes reactions to the flow of life experiences.

4. Progress in analysis should not be judged over too short a time period. Approximately every six months is a good interval to reflect on whether the analysis is on what seems to be a proper course.

5. The personal equation between the analyst and the patient is more important than the professional or theoretical background of the analyst.

6. Difficulties with the analysis should be discussed openly, since analyst and analysand are co-workers in helping the analysand with his or her own unconscious.

Portrait 1938, by Joan Miro.
(Kunsthaus, Zurich)

2

The Mind and the Body

We are so accustomed to feeling that we "have" a body (in contrast to *being* a body) that we seldom think of it. What we actually seem to "have" however is a body-image, a sense of our bodily existence in space. It is only in rare instances during waking life that we experience the difference between the actual body and our body-image. I remember the first time I looked in a mirror and realized that my once thick brown hair was thinning. Even further back, in early adolescence, I recall when I first noticed that my body had grown dark hair on the backs of my fingers. That reminded me of my father and made me feel that I was growing up.

There are instances, not rare, after amputations of an extremity, where the person still "feels" the missing part to be there. What is experienced is the body-image that seemed congruent with the amputated limb when it was still there. We once had a neighbor in his fifties who had lost the lower part of one leg when he was in his teens. He still felt he could wiggle his toes on the missing "phantom" limb.

In my psychiatric practice I have at times seen persons who have lost large amounts of weight, over a hundred pounds, and yet still feel fat, and there have been patients with anorexia who were thin as bed rails and still felt obese. The body-image is more enduring than the body, it seems, and the body-image exists in the mind.

Science assumes, by and large, that the body is primary and that the term "mind" is simply a word that designates our awareness when the body (particularly the brain) is working properly. In this view, called *epiphenomenalism*, the mind has no independent existence and would completely perish with the death of the body.

Other views are usually called *dualistic*—meaning that mind and body are somehow separate and separable entities, although it is impossible to specify the form that mind takes without the body and the brain, since in our observation they always occur together. It is difficult to categorize the Jungian position as clearly dualistic. It certainly emphasizes that such phenomena as synchronicity, ESP or extrasensory perception (telepathy, clairvoyance and precognition) do occur. These unusual events, to which Jung devoted a major work,[13] must be taken into account in a comprehensive view of the world.

Complexes: How They Form and How They Change

Just as there are images of the body in our minds, sometimes more enduring than the parts of the body they represent, there are other images as well. These are not randomly distributed, but are grouped into what Jung called *complexes*. The term complex has become so much a part of our ordinary language (as in, "He has a mother complex") that we seldom realize it has a more precise meaning. A psychological complex in Jungian theory is a group of related images having a common emotional tone and formed about an archetypal core.

Around the mother archetype, for example, a number of images may be related. Some of them clearly go together, such as an image of the personal mother, the personal grandmother, perhaps an older mothering sister, a school teacher, shading into figures from collective consciousness—a movie star, perhaps, or a female politician or minister, the queen of England or Mary Queen of Heaven. It is not too surprising when all the figures have a maternal meaning in relation to the ego, but it can be startling to find a mother complex active, for example, behind a man's relation to a male employer. I recall a young male patient who unconsciously kept expecting his boss to relate to him as his mother did, while the boss expected him to behave as an adult man.

Complexes are formed as experiences cluster about archetypal determinants. It is as if the archetypes form a magnetic field that differentially attracts and orders experiences. The archetypes in themselves are this ordering principle, while an image that stands for an archetype is called an *archetypal image*. Archetypal images, such as the hero, dragon, cross, treasure, etc., are typically found in mythology, religion and folklore. The figure of the witch, for instance, stands for a negative form of the mother archetype; appearing in an individual's dream it might point to an active negative mother complex. We can never know or experience the archetype itself, rather we experience an image of it or feel its activity in the way images are arranged, for instance in a fairy tale or a dream.

Complexes can separate or merge together. In fact, they are probably always in the process of such movement. It appears that dreams are often spontaneous pictures of the reworking of the complexes during sleep (see chapter 6). Complexes are assumed to be active, or constellated, when the mind is in a state of emotional arousal.

One of the most striking examples of the sudden formation of a complex, and its persistence over time, is the result of *traumatic neurosis*. Traumatic neurosis is caused by a person being helplessly caught in an overwhelming situation. A person pinned under a collapsed building, for example, or a soldier in combat unable to move because of enemy fire, may have a sense of complete helplessness and hopelessness. If the person survives, there often are recurrent dreams that exactly reproduce the traumatic situation. Such dreams may persist for years (more than twenty-five years in one case I knew). Freud, observing such traumatic combat dreams after the First World War, abandoned his concept of the pleasure principle as an exclusive determinant of mental contents and elaborated a parallel "death instinct."

It seems to me that complexes can also be formed spontaneously by the psyche, particularly during dreams.[14] There are rare instances, for example, in which a person awakens from a vivid dream with a strong image in mind, one that persists over time and has a significant impact on the person's subsequent life. One man dreamed that an authoritative voice said, "You are not living your true life!" In becoming concerned about the meaning of that dream, he reexamined himself over a period of several years, with the dream always in the back of his mind. The vivid image formed by the dream was the focal point of repeated reflection. Other ideas and images from the dreamer's life began to cluster around this memory of the dream. In structural language, many of the complexes in his mind were reevaluated and regrouped in new combinations. It did lead him toward a different basic arrangement of his life pattern.

There then appear to be two determinants in the formation of complexes. First is the experience of waking life, where a complex is likely to form if strong emotion is involved. Secondly, the action of the unconscious is involved, both in the usually slow formation of complexes through the archetypal field structuring ongoing experiences, and also through the rapid and spontaneous creation of a new complex structure, as in a dream. The action of the unconscious that can be observed more clearly in a dream also doubtless occurs during waking life as well, where it probably functions through a differential emotional meaning unconsciously attached to daily events.

It is important to remember that psychological complexes are not necessarily pathological, they are normal building blocks of the mind. Complexes determine to a great degree how we experience ourselves and others. They can be observed in personified form in dream images. And they can be demonstrated in the laboratory, as Jung did in his early work, in the word-association experiment and other psychological testing procedures.[15]

The Ego Complex

The ego itself, our subjective sense of "I," can be considered a complex, but one that is different from other complexes in that consciousness is associated with it. Any contents of the psyche that are closely attached to the ego, therefore, also partake of consciousness.

The ego complex seems to be based upon the central archetype of the *Self* in the objective psyche (or collective unconscious). The term Self as used by Jung means something far different from the "self" of ordinary language (as in "self-aware," "self-centered," "self-confident," etc.). The Self can also be called the central archetype of order. The archetypal Self is theoretically the center of the psyche as a whole (both consciousness and the unconscious), although the ego, which is actually only the center of consciousness, considers itself to be the center of the psyche. This is an illusion that is corrected as individuation proceeds.

The ego's mistaken sense that it is the center of the psyche has a parallel in the former collective belief that the earth was the center of the solar system. Another parallel occurs in Valentinian gnosticism, an early variant of Christianity, in which "god" was not the high god, but an intermediary who created an imperfect world but mistakenly considered himself the highest authority.

Dissolution of Complexes

Complexes change over time, according to one's experiences in life. But if all new experience is simply assimilated to existing complexes, nothing changes except that the complex gains more "weight," the psychic structure becoming ever more rigid. But there are spontaneous forces in the psyche, activated by the Self, that exert continual pressure toward the dissolution or depotentiation of pathological complexes while promoting order and growth in the service of individuation. This pressure toward individuation can be followed in a series of dreams, if seen from the classical Jungian perspective, and can be noted in life histories, where people often "outgrow" their earlier problems, frequently in their late forties or early fifties.

Dreams, too, seem to serve the reworking of complexes that make up the structure of the psyche, in order to promote the process of individuation. In the dreams typical of traumatic neurosis, for example, the traumatic situation may exactly recur for a long period, even years, before a symbolic change occurs in the recurrent dream, indicating that the traumatic complex is at last being metabolized, freeing the psyche of that particular sense of the ego being overwhelmed.

In the case mentioned above, where the traumatic dream had lasted more than twenty-five years, the original situation occurred during the Korean War. The dreamer had been in charge of a platoon of seventeen men who, against his own best judgment, were sent out on a dark rainy night on a scouting mission. They were ambushed, and only the dreamer and one other soldier escaped alive. For years, the dreamer would have nightmares so severe that he suggested to his wife that she sleep in another bedroom so he would not accidentally hit her if he awoke in terror from the nightmare. Gradually, the nightmares came at less frequent intervals, although almost without exception they occurred when the night was actually rainy. As he worked on himself, he reported, some twenty-five years after the event, that he experienced on a rainy night an unusual dream, having some of the elements of the original traumatic dream, but in an obviously changed form. Since that dream (now several years ago) the traumatic dream has not returned even on stormy nights.

The slow, natural dissolution of a complex can be speeded up considerably with successful Jungian analysis. There seem to be two components in such a process, both of which are important in different ways and at different times. The first is an understanding of the meaning of the complex, so that its "purpose" can be understood in consciousness. The second is to experience the complex with affect (emotion) while in a safe situation where the complex can be reflected upon in the light of the conscious values of the personality.

The Purpose and Experience of a Complex

An understanding of the apparent "purpose" of a complex may come through realizing how the complex originated in the life of the particular patient (through reconstruction of the past life); it may come in a symbolic mode (through dream interpretation and other symbolic procedures); or it may come in the observation of the patient in current situations where the complex can be identified as active (as in formal group psychotherapy or in just about any relationship).

It is important to remember that complexes behave as if they were part-personalities. Each complex has the potential of organizing an entire personality of greater or lesser complexity, analogous to the way in which each cell of the body contains the genetic information *in potentia* for the creation of an entire human organism. Of course, the complex is constrained to function as a part of the total organism, just as human body cells in the healthy state behave as orderly parts of the body. A cell unregulated to serve the good of the body as a whole becomes cancerous; a complex unrelated to the organization of the psyche (including both consciousness and the unconscious) can lead to neurosis or (in the worst case) psychosis.

When the ego of a person is "possessed" by a complex—that is to say when a complex is activated—the personality undergoes a marked change. One knows a complex has been activated (constellated) whenever one experiences an excess of emotion, whether it be anger or joy. The ego tends to identify with an active complex; in effect, the usual ego-image temporarily disappears and the complex takes over. Rarely, this can turn out to be for the good of the individual; more often it is a disaster.

If one can imagine that the complex has a rudimentary consciousness of its own, it is then possible to imagine that it has its own particular purpose. The complex may, in fact, from its viewpoint, feel that it knows what is best for the psyche as a whole. This is often evident when it is the shadow with which the ego temporarily identifies. Anyone who has had to deal with a loved family member who has an alcohol problem will think of ready examples. The usual personality virtually disappears with the ingestion of alcohol and is replaced by a relatively stable shadow personality that can be belligerent or fun-loving, or in some notable way different from the sober ego state. When the shadow personality is in ascendence, it "knows" things with certainty and adopts attitudes that may be at wide variance with the usual sober personality.

The shadow, or indeed any complex, if unrelated to the psyche as a whole, can be just as destructive and even life-threatening as a cancerous cell of the body that has escaped normal integration into the healthy systems of the body.

The Affect-Ego

Mere conscious awareness of a complex does little to alter its activity in the unconscious. After about seventy-five hours of analysis with my first analyst, Bingham Dai, he interpreted yet another dream in terms of my mother complex. With a slight degree of impatience, I said, "Dr. Dai, I *know* about my mother complex, can't we learn about something else?" I remember he laughed gently. Perhaps the most recent experience of my mother complex was yesterday morning, so it is still active and alive, but my relation to the complex now is vastly different from what it used to be.

What does alter a complex is for it to be active, with the emotional and affect charge that it carries, at the same time that there is the possibility for conscious reflection upon how it influences the psyche. This is one purpose of the formal *temenos* of the analytic sessions, which function as a safe place in which to examine our day-to-day emotional reactions. It is also what occurs naturally in many dreams: the dream-ego finds itself in an emotionally charged situation and must respond to it in some manner. The result of the action of the dream-ego (which in some dreams may consist of inaction or simply a change in emotional attitude) affects the way the complexes of the psyche are structured. The results are inherited by the waking-ego, often as a barely recognized change in emotional reactions or behavior patterns.

Jung introduced the term *affect-ego* to describe the ego of the person taking the word-association experiment when the ordinary ego was modified by the presence of affect associated with the complex.[16] Though apparently neglected by Jung once he introduced the term (it does not appear again in his writings), it has proven of great aid in conceptualizing and teaching the use of various models of psychotherapy to psychiatric residents and Jungian training candidates. It is also of significant value in following the changes that take place in the course of dyadic (two-person) interaction in analysis. The styles of useful intervention by the analyst are considerably broadened when the production of affect-ego states are considered as an important part of the analytical process. For example, some judicious use of the techniques of hypnotic age-regression, gestalt enactment techniques such as dialogue with absent parents, letters to persons who are deceased, etc., may be used in a coherent theoretical manner.

Much of psychotherapy is designed to help the patient safely experience affect-ego states associated with troublesome complexes. Some of these techniques are discussed in chapter 7 as variations of analysis. The concept of inducing and containing an affect-ego state helps to understand why many of these techniques are of value in the treatment of psychoneurosis. Of course, inducing and containing affect-ego states associated with complexes are what most of our dreams are already doing. But our conscious awareness of the dreams permits us to move at times faster in the direction they are seeking.

Group psychotherapy, when used in connection with Jungian analysis, is a powerful way of inducing and then working with affect-ego states. It also serves other functions, such as education and social example. In the closed and protected *temenos* of a properly-run therapy group, complexes are inevitably constellated and their effects noted. The correlation of the interpersonal observations in the group setting with similar complexes manifesting in dreams, together with an understanding of the origin of the complex in the history of the analysand, allow an increase in opportunities to both experience the complex and consciously reflect upon that experience in the light of more mature judgment.

Identity Structures

In attempting to explain the nature of the structural parts of the psyche from a Jungian standpoint, I have introduced the term *identity structures* to refer to the *ego* and the *shadow*, and the term *relational structures* to refer to the *persona* and the *anima/animus*. This terminology (see appendix 1) is meant to help keep in mind that what is developmentally cast into the shadow might just as well in different circumstances have become ego. Much of the shadow can be reworked in adult life and add dimension and contrast to the ego. The persona and the anima/animus remain always to some degree relational; they are bridges of relationship to the outer world (persona) and to the inner world (anima/animus), and serve the function of enlarging the personal sphere of activity of the ego, both in the outer ranges of collective consciousness and in the inner ranges of the personal unconscious.

All of these structural components of the psyche can be pictured as composed of various arrangements of complexes. A particular complex structure can exist at various times in the persona, in the ego or shadow, or in the anima or animus. In addition, complexes are related to each other and have something like statistically expectable reactions to certain other complexes. In their negative form, the anima and the animus have a classical interaction that is defensive rather than connecting, working against their natural function to enlarge the personal sphere and connect the ego with persons and situations (or depths of experience) previously outside its range of comfortable interaction. This is discussed to some extent in chapter 7, as it is of prime importance in the treatment of couples in marital therapy.

Such structural terms as anima/animus, shadow, ego and persona, therefore, are like molecular descriptions, while the complexes that are involved are analogous to the atoms that compose the molecules. As a change in the arrangement of the atoms may produce a molecule with different properties, so the rearrangement of complexes, the basic building blocks of the psyche, can greatly alter the ego's experience of itself and the world.

To clearly discuss clinical situations it has seemed to me necessary to introduce the term *ego-image*.[17] This is to permit a clear distinction between the image of the ego and the ego itself, which in its basic form consists of a center of subjectivity based on the archetype of the Self.

As this core of the ego identifies with certain structures of complexes, it gains a "from-to" structure.[18] The ego always experiences itself as identified with one pole of a multipolar pattern of complexes (an "object-relation pattern"). It then experiences *from* that pole of identification *to* other parts of the structure of that pattern of complexes. The complexes that are on the "to" side of the from-to structure may be experienced by the dream-ego as outside itself in the dream. In waking life, these same complexes may perhaps even be projected onto persons or situations in the external world.

For example, a person with an authoritarian complex usually has an identifiable bipolar structure of complexes: one pole is the "victim," the other the "victimizer." By projecting the victimizer pole of the authoritarian complex structure onto others, the possessor of such a complex will often feel victimized, even in situations that are neutral. Conversely, if placed in a position of power, the victim is likely to become the victimizer. True freedom from such an authoritarian complex releases the person from the danger of compulsively falling into *either* the role of the victim or the role of the victimizer. The integration of such a complex structure frees the person to both accept and respond to authority as the situation warrants, without feeling victimized *or* authoritarian.

One of the clearest ways of conceptualizing dreams is to see them as the Self creating a symbolic situation, usually from complexes at least partially in the ego-structure, and then offering the dream-ego an opportunity to alter that structure of complexes by its actions. Thus the dream-ego may be identified with only part of the complexes that constitute the waking-ego's tacit structure. Things in the dream that are external to the dream-ego may in the waking state even be a part of the tacit complex structure of the waking-ego itself.[19] A similar and unintentional shift in ego-boundaries during hypnosis was reported in the *Journal of the American Society of Clinical Hypnosis.*[20]

What I have referred to as structures of complexes might also be called *object-relation patterns*, since they serve to structure the relations of the ego to other object-patterns that are allowed by the constellated complex structure. For example, the classical oedipal complex admits of three different object-relation identities (father, mother and child), and also determines to a great degree the relations between those potential identities. The ego of a person with a strong oedipal pattern may at different times identify with one or more of the "persons" in the structure, which rather automatically assigns one of the remaining identities in the oedipal pattern to those persons with whom one has significant emotional interactions.

This extended discussion of identity structures may make it easier to understand a statement made in the introduction—that a person coming for analysis, although asking for change, has a hidden hope that he or she will be pronounced healthy and the problem lodged in external causes. *Whenever the present dominant ego-image is changing, the ego feels some threat of dissolution, even if the change is in the desired direction.* The ego in process of change seems to move from one identity (what I have called "dominant ego-image") toward another, usually more comprehensive, that is, the person is actually individuating. In all such change there is a transitional state where the old identity has been loosened and cannot be reinstated again, while the newer identity pattern has not yet been established firmly enough to feel secure. It is at this time of transition or liminality that the containing and protective quality of the analytic container is most crucial.

The term *liminality,* based on Victor Turner's description of traditional initiation rites, has come into some vogue in the United States to describe the sense of insecurity that accompanies significant psychological transformations of basic identity patterns.[21] During conditions that could be considered liminal, D.W. Winnicott's concept of the transitional object is of use,[22] as well as the natural emphasis on the *vas,* container, or boundary conditions of the treatment process. In one-to-one analytical interaction, the person of the analyst may function as a transitional object, but there are others—in group psychotherapy, it is frequently the group itself (useful when the analyst is carrying a strong projected role in an identity pattern that the patient is in the process of transcending).

Patients entering analysis can expect such periods of liminality. Being forewarned, perhaps they can transit such periods with less anxiety. What is always certain is that a new sense of a stable personality will arise. What is hoped for is that it will be in the direction of individuation and development, rather than what Jung called a *regressive restoration of the persona*, a move backward to an earlier personality organization that is inadequate to the present growth potential, but is secure (in a sense) because it is completely known.[23] The tendency toward such regression occurs at times in all of us; we feel it in yearnings for the security of the past, forgetting that the past is secure only because it is past; when the past was occurring it carried the same risks and states of liminality as the present.

Embodiment and Disembodiment: Dissolve and Coagulate

When the ego changes its identification with relatively stable complex structures, it changes its sense of identity in subtle ways, although the life history of the ego—the sense of continuity from childhood to the present—remains intact. Such change is by no means always easy, as witness the effort, both emotional and intellectual, that typically goes into analysis (for both analyst and analysand).

One can be caught in complexes from past experiences either because the past was exceptionally painful (and is still trying to be digested) or because it was excessively happy (and is still trying to be recaptured). The origin of the complex is the same in both cases—an emotionally-charged structure in the unconscious—but the emotion that created it may have been different. The common denominator lies not in the type of emotion, but in an unconscious attachment to the complex.

The actual clinical course of transcending a neurotic problem is frequently experienced as periods of time during which the old neurotic feelings are unchanged, alternating with periods that seem relatively free from the neurotic conflict. Gradually, sometimes without conscious awareness, it seems as if the new identity becomes solidified and is then the rule rather than the exception. It is well to remember this fluctuating pattern as the normal course of things, for it will then not be so disappointing when there is a period of regression to old ways. When one is finally out of a neurotic conflict, to look back at it creates wonder as to how one ever could have been so blind (or mistaken, or immature, etc.). Once a neurotic conflict is clearly transcended, it is much more difficult to regress, simply because it is not possible to see the terms of the conflict in the same neurotic manner. Growth involves a complete perceptual change.

The liminal fluctuation between old and new can be viewed in structural terms as the ego successively identifying and disidentifying with certain patterns of complexes. This can sometimes be seen dramatically in dreams or in interpersonal situations. In alchemical imagery, in which Jung found striking parallels to the psychological process of individuation, there is a dictum to "dissolve and coagulate" repeatedly. In another alchemical operation, taking place in a "pelican" (closed vessel), a material is repeatedly vaporized and sublimated in a circular process. These are projected archetypal images of repeated identification and disidentification with patterns of complexes during the liminal state, the state that is intermediate between old and new identities when the psyche is undergoing transformation. It should be endured with some degree of good humor, for it means one is making progress.

The Ego and the Self

The reality that is described by the theoretical relationship between the ego and the archetypal Self is one of the most mysterious in all of human experience. It is paradoxical. In one sense the ego is the Self, at least that part of the Self that exists in empirical consciousness, acting and living in the world of consensual reality. But in an equally profound sense, the ego is as subordinate to the Self as man is to God in traditional theological terms. As already mentioned, the archetypal Self is quite a different concept from the uncapitalized "self" of everyday usage in such phrases as "I am not myself today."

One of the pathological ways in which the archetypal Self is experienced is where there is a delusion of grandeur, the ego being identified with an image of the Self, as in the classic cartoon illustration of a person believing he is Napolean, Christ or some other important cultural hero. A number of these pathological experiences of the archetypal Self were reported when there was widespread use of LSD and other hallucinogenic drugs: it seemed as if the drug effect so weakened the ordinary ego structure that it identified with a grandiose aspect of the underlying archetype of the Self.

Another pathological form of the ego when it identifies with the archetypal Self under the influence of hallucinogenic drugs is for the ego to feel that it is God. This inflationary identity results from the ego losing its usual sense of a dominant ego-image, so that the archetypal image of the Self, the core of the ego, appears in consciousness as a mistaken ego-identity. When I was a psychiatrist in the army, at the height of the drug culture in the United States, a number of recruits who took such drugs as LSD told me that their primary problem was this: they *knew* from the drug experience that God was their true identity, and the drill sergeant did not understand that! God should not be assigned to K.P. ("kitchen patrol").

I always explained to them that even if it were true that they *were*

God, it was likely that the drill sergeant, the lieutenant, the captain of their company and even the commanding general of the post were also God. If it was a common denominator, perhaps it would be best to ignore it and adapt to the situation. If they could not do that, I suggested, perhaps they would have to be "God" on the psychiatric ward.

This approach convinced all but one young soldier to abandon (or at least not talk about) being God. The exception was a young man of low intelligence who should probably not have been inducted into the army in the first place. He had always been at the bottom of every pecking order, the last chosen for the baseball team—in other words, always on the periphery of being accepted. Nothing in his life, past or present, could compare to his feeling that he was God. He chose to hold on to this idea and did not mind at all maintaining it while on the psychiatric ward.

There are different ways of talking about the relation of the ego and the Self. Edward Edinger has called it an *ego-self axis*.[24] Moku-sen Miyuki speaks of an *eccentric ego,* an ego that is in some sense "to the side" of the usual ego.[25] The term I myself prefer is *ego-Self spiration,* to emphasize that there is a continual flow between ego and Self, the basic reality lying in the fluctuation and mutual interaction between them. Perhaps there is no better description than Jung's own—that in individuation the center of the personality moves from the ego toward the Self, establishing a new center of the psyche somewhere between the two.

In usual clinical practice, the concept of the Self does not need to be stressed. It exists in three ways: 1) as the archetypal core and template of the ego; 2) as a way of pointing toward the tendency of the psyche to form a coordinated whole; and 3) as an image of that tendency toward order that often can be seen in symbolic form as a mandala structure in dreams or imaginal productions. Mandala, traditionally a Buddhist meditation symbol, was the term chosen by Jung to refer to these ordered images that emphasize a periphery and a center, sometimes a four-gated city, or Christ surrounded by the four apostles, or the Egyptian mandala of Horus and his four sons.

Jung pointed to a particular contemporary problem—that spontaneously created modern mandalas seem often to have an empty center, with no god-figure as in traditional mandala forms.[26] This observation is open to many interpretations, but may mean that mankind must now come to terms with an image of God that does not have a clear form. Perhaps the movements toward Buddhist-Christian dialogue point in this direction.[27]

The sense of dialogue that develops in working with a series of dreams in Jungian analysis gives one an actual awareness of underlying order and meaningful process, a sense of the archetypal Self. The Self is theoretically the maker of dreams, and the analyst may ask pointedly why the Self selected one sort of dream sequence rather than another, one character to represent a complex rather than another, etc. The intuitive sense is that the Self is a center of consciousness that is older and wiser than the ego, but somehow dependent upon the ego for activity in the "real" world. From following thousands of dreams of many people over several decades, it is my own view that the Self is like a very wise, very compassionate friend, always concerned to help, but never coercive or excessively judgmental, and possessed of almost infinite patience.

The Psyche and the Soul

The psyche is the total world of conscious and unconscious mental life. No one knows its limits. It contains our models of the external world. Complexes are the building blocks of the personal part of the psyche, and archetypes are the great primordial patterns of the objective psyche (the collective unconscious). Complexes (and our identity based upon them) alter in the process of individuation, under the pressure of the Self toward actualizing our innate potentialities. Individuation is a direction, not a goal that is attained in this life. The most we can do, writes Jung, is to "dream the myth onwards," realizing that "whatever explanation and interpretation does to it, we do to our own souls as well."[28]

Jung called the anima and animus "soul images," because when the ego is out of touch with them it can feel like the state that in some primitive religious systems is called "loss of soul."[29] The soul is a connecting function, conveying a meaning that is deeper and more comprehensive than the ego ordinarily experiences. If the anima or animus is projected onto a person with whom one falls in love, then the absence of that person may feel like one has lost one's soul.

But the soul image can also be attached to things other than persons: to a cause, to a purpose, to one's country, etc.—even to objects (as in fetishes). The soul image gives a sense of meaningful connection beyond oneself, or at least the possibility of such connection. It is a sense of direction intimately concerned with the individuation process. Like all senses, it can be mistaken in its goal and it can miscarry. It is part of the work of analysis to keep one in touch with this dynamism of the psyche as seen from other perspectives, including the meaning of dreams.

Summary

1. We not only inhabit bodies, we inhabit structures of our minds. These structures determine our sense of identity, and when they are in the process of change we may experience disorientation, or a sense of liminality.

2. Complexes, the structures of the personal part of the psyche, are formed as the residue of emotion acting within the archetypal organizing field. To undo or transform those that are pathological, it is frequently necessary to reexperience the emotion attached to the complex, but in a safe and containing situation such as the analytic *temenos*.

3. The coordinating center of the entire psyche is the Self, which is also the archetypal model of the ego.

3

A Note About Diagnosis

When a person first visits a Jungian analyst (or any other therapist) there is a natural tendency to want to know what is "wrong." This is because we automatically tend to think in terms of a medical model: diagnosis (what is wrong), prognosis (what is the likely outcome) and treatment (what can be done to make things better).

If you are applying for insurance coverage to help cover the cost of analysis, a diagnosis is required by the insurance carrier. Insurance may or may not cover Jungian analysis, depending upon the diagnosis and the basic clinical degree of the analyst. Sometimes an insurance policy will cover analysis by a nonmedical analyst if the analysis is supervised by someone with medical credentials.

While the actual psychological state of a person is invariably more complex than can be covered in any system of diagnoses (hence many Jungians are loathe to give a formal diagnosis), some agreed-upon diagnostic categories are useful.

The system in current use is the Diagnostic and Statistical Manual III (DSM-III), worked out by a committee of the American Psychiatric Association. It replaces an earlier version of diagnostic categories—the DSM-II, which was based largely on Freudian psychoanalytic theory, but influenced also by other theories, such as the "reaction" model of Adolph Meyer.[30] The objection to DSM-II (which is also still in use) was this theoretical bias and the fact that it did not specify the signs and symptoms of a diagnosis sufficiently to facilitate research on competing explanations of mental disorder, for instance the psychodynamic and the neurophysiological.

When DSM-III was in preparation, the Inter-Regional Society of Jungian Analysts and several other Jungian groups communicated with the committee to protest the proposed diagnosis of "introverted personality." The Jungian objection was that *introvert* and *extravert,* terms which Jung introduced in his theory of psychological types, are equivalent—if there is a pathological diagnosis called "introverted personality" there would also be one called "extraverted personality"—but neither introvert nor extravert are pathological terms; they simply describe a normal attitudinal preference to locate basic values outside (extravert) or inside (introvert). The DSM-III committee was concerned and helpful, substituting the term "withdrawn personality" for the problem they were trying to describe.

The DSM-III categories currently in use were designed to be theoretically neutral, describing diagnostic categories as syndromes (symptoms that are found together). By specifying the component symptoms (the patient's complaints) and signs (things observable about the patient), it is possible to better design research about the psychiatric syndromes. This is good for research, but not terribly useful for the clinician.

Some clinical syndromes frequently seen by Jungians are not easily described in terms of DSM-III. The syndrome of the puer, for example, is frequently observed by Jungian analysts as a coherent grouping of symptoms that imply a certain cause, a probable course of treatment and a likely outcome. *Puer aeternus* is Latin for "eternal boy." (The proper feminine form is *puella,* but the term puer is often used to refer to the syndrome occurring in either sex.) The puer syndrome is characterized by a tendency to live in a world of possibilities, but to hold back from the work required to actualize them in outer life—largely because failure would damage the puer's self-image and be too painful to bear. Thus the puer tends to be caught in "the provisional life."[31] Peter Pan is a literary image of the puer, as is Saint-Exupery's *The Little Prince.*[32] Jungians may disagree about the archetypal imagery behind the puer, some emphasizing the image of the mother, others that of the father, but most would agree on the general description of the syndrome.

While the puer syndrome has many similarities to the diagnostic category *narcissistic personality,* there are significant differences. The puer description carries with it the implication that there exists within the person potentially positive qualities that ideally would be incorporated by the conscious ego through a process of differentiation and integration. It is characteristic of Jungian clinical thinking that disorders that bring a person to analysis also contain seeds of new and creative developments in the individuating personality. The goal is usually not just to "overcome" the presenting symptoms, but also to find and integrate their meaning.

There is a clear need to relate such Jungian concepts as the puer syndrome to more widely used categories of diagnosis in order to bring Jungian thought to the awareness of a wider circle of psychotherapists. While humanistic psychology has popularized many areas of Jungian concern, it has not been concerned with either the shadow or other archetypal aspects of the unconscious to any significant extent.

The relativity of diagnosis does not mean that diagnosis is unimportant in Jungian analysis. It is important in any psychotherapeutic undertaking, both as a signpost of the initial situation and as a way of gradually accumulating data about the same diagnosis among groups of people—a primary purpose of DSM-III. There is a need for creative research in Jungian clinical concepts. This is already underway in questions of typology (see below), with the Singer-Loomis typological profile abandoning the forced choice of opposite functions (thinking *or* feeling, sensation *or* intuition).[33]

Psychopathology and Individuation

Psychopathology (what is wrong with a person) and its cure is too narrow a framework to contain the goal of Jungian analysis, because many persons who benefit most from Jungian analysis have nothing diagnostically "wrong" in a clinical sense. Jung emphasized that the goal of life is *individuation*. By that term he meant something more profound and more comprehensive than is meant by its use in child development, where it refers to the psychological separation of the infant from the mother.[34]

Individuation is the manifestation in life of one's innate, inborn potentialities. Not all the possibilities can be realized, so individuation is never complete. It is more a quest than a goal, more a direction of movement than a resting place. The individuating ego comes again and again to points where it must transcend its previous image of itself. This is painful, for the ego continually identifies with images of itself, believing that the image with which it is presently identified is the "real" person. Thus the answers to the classic question, "Who am I?" are constantly open to modification.

The complete manifestation of a part of the potentiality, however, may inhibit the manifestation of another, equally important part. What is consistent with one ego-image may stand in the way of a larger, more comprehensive ego-image that is trying to form in the course of individuation. This frequently poses moral dilemmas: loyalty to the present good may inhibit and destroy the future greater good. To further complicate matters, there is no guarantee that the present ego-image can clearly be aware of the next developing ego-image. When the present ego-image attempts to imagine the future path of individuation, it may project it's own unintegrated complexes, even an ego-ideal from the persona, into the future.

Many neurotic symptoms are caused by the ego's attempting to hold back from a needed development in the individuation process of the person. If one holds back from learning to express normal assertiveness, for example, a clinical picture of depression often develops. On the surface it may appear that the depression is caused by outer events. Only with analytical understanding can one see that it is rather (or also) a question of becoming aware of and integrating one's potentialities. From a Jungian point of view, then, it is usually important to "go through" the depression to the other side, living through the inner conflict to a resolution, not just dealing with the symptoms of the depression until they are ended. There are impressive reports that this same treatment approach can be used creatively in schizo-affective disorders and possibly in even more severe forms of mental illness.[35]

This approach of "going through" the depression rather than repressing it or only treating the symptoms does not mean that one simply endures the suffering. Rather, one participates in it. In neurotic and characterological problems, in a real sense oneself *is* the illness. Getting rid of the symptoms without deeper inner change is like getting rid of a fever but leaving the infection that caused it unaltered. The attitude of growth and integration, however, conflicts with the current emphasis on the most rapid and least costly treatment of syndromes. In practice this shows up as limits that insurance will pay for the treatment of certain diagnoses. Often the insurance will cover treatment only until the major symptoms are corrected. The long-term cost of understanding the depth of meaning behind the symptoms is often borne by the patient alone.

Individuation is ultimately a mysterious process that leads naturally into questions of religion and the meaning of life. Jung described it as a process of circumambulation, circling around an unknown center of ourselves. The existence and evolution of life depends upon maintaining a dynamic relationship with this center of value and meaning.

In ordinary experience, we may be dimly aware of a deep background sense of meaning to our lives. At other times, it may seem as if we are estranged from this sense of meaningful order. But the existence of a meaningful order is implied in both our circumambulation of it and our estrangement from it. Edinger has suggested that the sense of approach and estrangement alternate in a cyclical manner along the "spiral" path of individuation.[36]

Individuation is the term used in Jungian psychology to describe the process by which the potentialities of a particular psyche unfold in the course of a life history. The history is always only a partial expression of the possibilities, so that individuation is never complete. The individuation process is experienced by the ego as a sense of being more or less "on track" in life. Dreams are in the service of the individuation process, as opposed to furthering the intentions of the ego; the ego often feels itself as moving in an unsuitable direction when it is overidentified with certain complexes or in the grip of an archetypal image toward which it has taken a too passive ego-stance.

Individuation is like continually spiraling about our real center, never being able to come to it directly, but always aware of whether we are moving toward or away from it. The individuation process is like an inner sense of direction that can be ignored or overridden, but not abandoned. Socrates's *daimon* was something like the sense of individuation, telling him when he was doing something wrong, but never telling him the "right" direction to move—that was the work of the ego.

The spiral is an excellent symbol for the path of individuation, because it combines the sense of movement along an inner axis with the image of circumambulating a center. If one imagines a line along one side of a spiral form, and pictures the ego as moving along it, we have a sense of the way in which one continually comes back to the same problems (like my previously mentioned mother complex) but at a different level with each turn of the spiral. To paraphrase T.S. Eliot, in *Four Quartets,* it is like finding that our end was in our beginning, but we come to know it for the first time.

Many apparently pathological symptoms can be seen from an analytic point of view as substitutes for a needed step in individuation that the patient has tried to avoid. The avoidance of integrating normal levels of aggression, for instance, may simultaneously make one oversensitive to aggressiveness in others and, if continued, may lead to depression. The depression is the presenting symptom, and it may be "explained" in terms of the aggressiveness of others, but the underlying meaning is the need for integration of the patient's own assertiveness.

We return to an earlier insight: the reason that a person comes for Jungian analysis may be the "wrong" reason. Analysis may be the right path, but the real reason for being involved in it usually evolves and develops during the course of the analysis. Ultimately, the reason or motivation is individuation, becoming more and more the person that one potentially is.

A new person in group psychotherapy, for instance, is often concerned with how long others have been in the group, frequently focusing upon the member who has been there longest and complaining, "I can't stay *that* long!" What is not realized is that the reasons a person remains in therapy for an extended period of time are usually quite different from those that brought one in the first place.

Individuation is a natural process that goes on in everyone. Jungian analysis does not produce the individuation process, but it can often activate it, make it more conscious and accelerate the speed at which it occurs. There are three major differences between a person who is individuating in a natural way or through an analytical experience. The person whose individuation has been stimulated through analysis is 1) more able to consciously grasp and describe the process, 2) less likely to regress into neurotic behavior patterns, and 3) more able to help another (as "midwife") through the same process. This is not to say, however, that one way of individuating is superior to the other. They are simply different. Humans were experiencing individuation in various ways and to varying depths long before Jung used the term as we do today.

Individuation is so personal a process, so unlike the broad generalizations of what is "normal" or "healthy" in a given society, that we must always respect its very personal nature. If life were endless, one could say that everyone would individuate to a virtually complete degree, even if it took hundreds or thousands of years. Perhaps there is continuation of life beyond death, either on another plane of existence or through repeated incarnations. But from our mortal human vantage point all we can observe is that there is a deep and enduring quest within the psyche of each of us to move inexorably, albeit with many false steps, toward our own larger selves. This movement may appear "pathological" from the point of view of any self-identity that we have already achieved, although it may in fact be the saving transformation that is needed in our lives.

So personal indeed is this movement, that not even an analyst who is well acquainted with one's process can be sure that a move out of a current pattern is in the service of individuation or not. We must always struggle with our own regressive tendencies and our inescapable desires to rationalize our less worthy motives as if they were higher goals. Life is always a risk, but one that we are free to take in various ways—the choices by which we weave the potentialities of our lives into our own distinctive pattern.

When you are truly embedded in an analytical relationship, you can expect that your analyst will stay with you through these decision nodes and their consequences. At its best, analysis helps such nodal decisions to be made with as little disruption as possible, both to the person in analysis and to those with whom the analysand is in relationship. The solution is always personal. The analyst, like Socrates's *daimon,* is better able to help you realize when a particular move would be false or unsuitable than what the "right" step would be. Sometimes the fear of making a change, or the fear of being overinfluenced by the analyst, tempts a person to interrupt analysis prematurely. This problem is discussed in chapter 5.

Psychological Types

Jung based his system of typology, for which he is perhaps most widely recognized at present, on an extensive historical review of the type question in literature, mythology, aesthetics, philosophy and psychopathology. His scholarly research and a lengthy summary of his conclusions were first published in 1921. A number of widely used type tests are now based upon Jungian principles: the Myers-Briggs, the Gray-Wheelwright, the Singer-Loomis, and several others that have been developed for specific research purposes.

Jung initially elaborated his theory of typology in order to explain how he, Freud, Adler and others could hold such differing views about the same clinical material.[37] Jung concluded that they interpreted the relevant facts quite differently because of variations in the way they functioned psychologically, that is, their personal typology.

In Jung's model, there are two major attitudinal types: *extraver-*

sion and *introversion*. These terms have become famous and are part of the cultural knowledge of most educated persons, although few people outside the field of psychology realize that they originated in Jung's work. The primary difference between extraversion and introversion is that in extraversion there is an outward movement of interest *toward the object,* while in introversion the movement of interest is away from the outer object and *toward the subject.*[38] Although interest is often in the same direction as the person's activities—an extravert being more active in the external world and an introvert showing more internal activity—the primary indication of extraversion and introversion is based on the *direction of interest,* not the direction of activity.

Extraversion and introversion, speaking generally, also can be used to describe cultures. American culture, for example, is *in general* more extraverted than the Swiss culture, which tends to be introverted. Jolande Jacobi, one of Jung's early interpreters, said that when visiting America she was considered very introverted, but at home in Switzerland she was thought of as a wild extravert—exemplifying the cultural relativity of such judgments.

Functional Types

In addition to the major orientation of the personality as extraverted or introverted, Jung described four functions, which in combination yield a finer description of personality typology. The four functions are *thinking, feeling, intuition* and *sensation.*[39]

Thinking and feeling are called "rational" functions because it is possible to order events and attitudes with either of them. With the thinking function, material is ordered according to a logical pattern ("A logically precedes B"); with the feeling function, material is ordered according to its feeling-tone value ("I am more interested in relationship A than in relationship B").

The feeling function is *not* equivalent to emotion or affective response. Emotion can vary more rapidly than feeling and is developed from the context of a situation; feeling is a value judgment and can be used in a more dispassionate manner. In fact, a person whose primary function is feeling may at times appear "cold" because she or he may respond more to the underlying feeling value of a situation rather than to the immediate emotion.

Intuition and sensation are called "irrational" functions. In this context, "irrational" does not mean *against* rationality, but simply indicates that these two functions—unlike thinking and feeling—do not offer a framework for ordering experiences. Instead, they are ways of perceiving: sensation perceives through the physical senses, while intuition is perception through the unconscious.

The sensation function tells one *what is*. When applied to physical objects, it is the function that notices such things as the number of items, the names, colors and other particularities. In Rudyard Kipling's famous novel *Kim*, the boy-hero was taught observational skills by being briefly shown a tray of small objects and then asked to remember and describe them. This game developed his sensation function, which excels at detail.

Intuition, the other "irrational" function, does not tell one what *is*, but rather *what are the potential outcomes*, the possibilities, of a given situation. Intuition has a probabilistic and predictive quality. When we anticipate the meaning of what a person is saying to us we are using the intuitive function. Sometimes intuition leaps far ahead of the spoken words and anticipates quite accurately, but sometimes it is mistaken. People who rely primarily on the intuitive function often have difficulty tolerating a slow pace of events; such impatience can interfere with the orderly or natural unfolding of a conversation or relationship.

Activity of the Functions

The two attitudinal types and the four functions can be separated only conceptually. In actual persons, they always act in concert. Since one function usually is developed to a far greater degree than the others, a person entering a new and unfamiliar situation in life will tend to approach it with his or her best (*primary* or *superior*) function. There is usually also a relatively well-developed secondary function which acts in congruence with the primary function. The least developed function is usually called the *inferior* function, meaning that it is more unconscious and not easily available to the ego.

For that reason, the process of individuation often requires that the inferior function be developed. For example, in fairy tales, which can be seen as a model for ego-development, the inferior function is often represented by the "dumbling" son, the naive youngest brother whom everyone despises, but who is close to the unconscious natural world, able to speak with the animals and follow the deeper, irrational but essential processes of nature.

When tired, intoxicated or simply pressed beyond normal limits, the range of adaptation of the superior function may be exhausted and other functions, possibly the inferior function, come into play. In the famous television series *Star Trek,* the central characters approximate the four functions: Mr. Spock is primarily the thinking function, Dr. McCoy the feeling function, Scotty the engineer is sensation, while Captain Kirk as the intuitive function takes final responsibility in irrational and dangerous situations.

Typology and Analysis

Because the four functions and the two attitudinal types represent one model of the totality of psychic functioning, the goal of individuation can be phrased in terms of typology. In a general sense, individuation is furthered by the development of the inferior function, as well as the development of the opposite attitudinal type— introverts developing their extraverted side and vice versa. In Western culture it is natural in the first half of life to emphasize an extraverted mode, for at this stage the psyche presses for the establishment of a strong ego in the outer world. Conversely, introversion is a more natural mode in the second half of life, when the goal is not to establish oneself in the world, but to assess the meaning of one's life in preparation for death.

Jungian analysis speeds up the process of psychological development, attempting to produce the results of individuation in a shorter time than would naturally occur. Because of this pressure for more intentional psychological development, analysis is, like alchemy, a "work against nature." The goal is the same as the natural goal, metaphorically the production of the *lapis* or Philosophers' Stone, but the intentionality of the process meets resistance from the slower pace of most unconscious processes.

Some Jungian analysts make great use of typology as a basic guide to the orientation of the analytical process. I personally do not. In my own practice I make an assessment of typology at the beginning of the analysis, often using one or more of the type tests to confirm my clinical impressions. The developing process of the analysis, however, always seems more basic and personal than the typological description. On the other hand, I have found typology useful in helping analysands understand some of their difficulties (like being an extreme introvert in an extraverted environment, or using the thinking function when feeling or intuition would be more appropriate).

Typology is also quite helpful in counseling some couples, for communication problems can easily arise between two persons who are of very different types; in such instances, an understanding of the other's way of functioning can often alleviate the situation and facilitate harmonious interaction.

Summary

1. The diagnosis of a mental problem is always relative and less complex than the actual person it describes.

2. Many syndromes of concern to Jungians are not easily diagnosed in terms of the current categories of DSM-III.

3. The process of individuation, the basic process of human life, may produce symptoms of psychological disturbance when necessary stages of growth are resisted.

4. Analysis can help to differentiate the situations that produce the symptoms, and may help the analysand to move more rapidly through the nodal point where the individuation process is interrupted by symptoms.

5. Individuation, a spiral process of circumambulating the core of our true being, is a direction more than an attainable goal. It is of a very personal nature and cannot be adequately described by general norms of health and illness.

6. A basic knowledge of psychological typology can be helpful in understanding one's personal difficulties and relationship problems.

Two paintings by a woman in Jungian analysis: *bottom*, a state of depression in which unconscious contents are activated but repressed; *top*, conflict and confusion after the unconscious contents have become conscious.

4

The Structure of Analysis

Upon first entering Jungian analysis, most people have an expectation, conscious or unconscious, that 1) the analyst will help them solve the problem that motivated them to come for analysis, or 2) there will be an exploration of past life, particularly childhood memories.

The first expectation, relief of symptoms, is a natural human desire. The second, exploration of the past as a way of relieving distress in the present, is based upon a widespread acceptance of a stereotype of Freudian psychoanalysis—that everything can be traced back to childhood experiences or fantasies.

Jung called the tracing of present difficulties to events of the past *reductive analysis,* since it "reduced" the present difficulty to something else. Jung never repudiated reductive analysis, and indeed felt that in some cases it was the best approach, certainly for those persons whose problems could clearly be seen as deriving from earlier difficulties. Jung focused, however, as do most Jungian analysts, upon a clearer understanding of what the unconscious mind is already trying to do to help the person out of the difficulty. This activity of the unconscious mind can be seen with particular clarity in dreams, which are discussed in chapter 6.

A particular Jungian analyst might begin by taking a detailed history, perhaps with some psychological tests, including studies such as sandtray projections, a technique that is employed by many Jungians but seldom by other therapists. Another analyst might simply start working with the problem where it manifests, letting the past history develop as the analysis proceeds.

There are also, as previously mentioned, wide variations in the physical arrangement within which analysis occurs. The usual procedure is for analyst and analysand to sit face to face, although some Jungian analysts, particularly those trained in the developmental school (largely in England), may ask that the patient lie on a couch, much as in classical Freudian analysis. Use of the couch promotes controlled regression, but there are differences of opinion as to its usefulness.[40]

Frequency and Fees

The frequency of analytic sessions may also vary widely. While analysts of the developmental school may ask analysands to come three or four times each week, the usual frequency for Jungians is once or twice weekly. This, too, may be adjusted according to the severity of the symptoms. A crisis situation may occur in the patient's life (from outer *or* inner events), making more frequent sessions desirable.

I myself find that once or twice a week is quite workable for most people, while a frequency of less than twice a month tends to lose the continuity of the analysis. When an analysand is simultaneously in group psychotherapy with the analyst, it is often possible to decrease the frequency of individual analytical appointments (although this option is limited by the rarity of Jungian analysts who also do group psychotherapy).

Fee schedules vary among analysts, and from one part of the country to another, so they must be negotiated on an individual basis. Some analysts offer sliding fee scales, particularly for students or when just beginning practice. In some places, such as New York and San Francisco, the local Jungian institute maintains a clinic where analysis is available from training candidates at reduced fees. Some analysts charge differing fees for longer or shorter sessions.

Many analysts request payment at the time of each visit, while others bill on a monthly basis. It is important to be realistic about what can be afforded. In general, as suggested earlier, it is better to be in an on-going analysis of less frequency for a longer time, then intensively for a limited period of time. In all cases, the fee structure is an important part of the contract between analyst and analysand and should be perfectly clear at the beginning. Any misunderstandings should be immediately addressed, although they may be handled as analytic material as well as part of the contractual arrangement.

Many unconscious meanings attach to money, such as self-worth ("No one cares about me if I don't pay"), sacrifice ("I'm giving up buying a new car to afford analysis"), bodily substance ("Money is shit") and energy ("What I spend money on shows where my energy wants to go"). I know of at least one instance in which a new analysand spent the first session talking to his analyst about whether he should pay the analyst or the analyst should pay him! (He finally agreed to pay the analyst.) Most of us would unconsciously like to think that we are so important to our analysts that they would see us whether we paid or not, while knowing consciously that it is a professional arrangement and fees are appropriate.

Value received for payment is also an important question, particularly since there are often times when the analysand may wonder if he is "progressing" or "getting anywhere." Such questions frequently reveal an uncertain sense of one's own self-worth, or a desire to have insecurities swept away by the approval of a strong authority figure, the analyst being appropriated for that purpose. But what is analysis actually worth? Is it necessary to pay someone "just to listen"?

When I was in psychiatric training, a professor told our resident group the sanest thing I have yet heard about fees. Many of us were hesitant to begin charging patients when we went into practice, knowing our own limitations and insecurities. The professor said that the fee one charges does not necessarily correspond to one's value to the patient. The fee only indicates the amount of money for which one is willing to do psychotherapeutic work. If the therapist helps the patient out of a severe problem, the hourly fee is cheap for the results achieved. If there are no substantial results, the analyst may not be worth a nickel an hour. Since no one can know the outcome of the treatment, the real meaning of the fee is, as the professor said, the wage for which one is willing to work.[41]

Missed Appointments

It is routine to charge monthly for group psychotherapy, even if the patient misses a meeting. What is paid for is a place in the group, which belongs to the patient and cannot be offered to someone else. Individual time is a different matter. Many analysts permit cancellation of appointments with sufficient notice, usually twenty-four or forty-eight hours. The open time may then be offered to someone else, or the analyst may plan to use the time for personal purposes. Some few analysts make a clear contract with the new patient that a particular hour is reserved for the patient for a set period of time or until they mutually agree otherwise. If such an arrangement is made, missed appointments are charged.

In all cases of missed appointments there is likely to be some underlying psychodynamic reason. It may be that the topic under discussion at the end of the previous meeting had more emotional meaning than was realized, and the analysand unconsciously wanted to avoid discussion of it again. Most analysts charge for missed appointments simply on the basis of whether the time was canceled far enough in advance. Although there may be psychodynamic reasons, or very practical ones ("My car wouldn't start," "I had to take my son to the dentist," etc.), I myself do not want to be in a position of deciding what is a valid or invalid reason for missing an appointment.

Years ago a physician missed his appointment with me without calling to cancel. I charged him a nominal amount (less than half his usual fee), although we had agreed that uncanceled appointments would be charged at full rate. In our next meeting he spent the first half of the time arguing that I should not have charged him at all, because he had missed his appointment for what he considered a valid reason. I would not change my position, pointing out that our agreement was to give me at least twenty-four hours' notice, not to provide a good reason for not showing up. He became very angry. At the midpoint of the session, I decided to drop the late-cancellation charge because I sensed there was a deeper underlying issue.

When I told him I would cancel the late charge, he suddenly burst into tears. A deep neurotic structure emerged—he felt no one cared for him, but only for what he paid or could do for them. He was so convinced of his personal worthlessness that he had never dared to mention those feelings, even in analysis. The energy generated by his affect, and my sudden cancellation of the charge, caught his defense system off guard.

Clearly, fees are more than fees. They also carry emotional meaning.

Boundary Conditions: The Therapeutic Contract

Such things as fees, frequency of appointments, etc., constitute an agreement between analyst and analysand as between two adults making a contract. Such contractual arrangements are the boundary conditions of analysis. They mark off the analytical relationship from other parts of life, so that the interaction within those boundaries can be used for the special purpose of understanding the patient's unconscious functioning.

The choice of particular boundary conditions has some effect on what can be observed within them. Analysts who see patients several times a week, with the patient often lying on a couch, frequently state that such an arrangement allows observations that cannot be seen in once-a-week, face-to-face sessions. Others (myself included) feel that simultaneous group psychotherapy and individual analytical sessions with the same therapist allow a range of observation not possible in individual sessions alone. Virtually all Jungian analysts agree that the interpretation of dreams adds a dimension to analysis that cannot be achieved by other means.

Some therapists, following R.D. Langs, refer to boundary conditions as the *frame* of the analysis.[42] The frame is a good visual image, since we are immediately aware that when something is framed it is both emphasized and separated from its surroundings. The frame also restricts what one can observe, which permits a selection process of the type of material studied. Most importantly, once a frame or boundary condition is established by mutual agreement, deviations from it can be interpreted as acts that are consciously or unconsciously meaningful. Usually it is a case of the analyst interpreting the patient's deviations from the boundary conditions, but the analyst may also act outside the frame (as in being late for or forgetting an appointment) and that may be equally revealing.

After what seemed a routine session with a patient I had seen in analysis for several years, he came to the next appointment reporting (not showing) that he had experienced a great deal of anger at me for not giving him the full time on his last session, believing I had shortened his visit by two minutes. He was accusing me of having deviated from the boundary conditions. What he had come to realize, though, was that he was trying to make me a positive father, like his previous analyst, to make up for his negative experience with his own natural father. That was a significant and long-overdue insight that proved most useful to him in his analysis. It was actually unclear if I had cut his time short by two minutes. I believed I had not, but I had measured the time of his previous session by one of two clocks in my office, while he had judged it by the other. When we compared the clocks they were exactly two minutes apart in time! The unresolvable question of the two minutes was insignificant compared to the new insight he had gained.

The boundary conditions of Jungian analysis are often referred to in the literature as the *vas* (or *vas bene clausum,* the "well-closed vessel"). This is a reference to the archetypal image of the alchemical vessel, the glass container within which the dross, the *prima materia,* was to be transformed into the Philosophers' Stone. One such *vas,* mentioned previously, was called a pelican because it resembled that bird with its head on its breast (also a medieval symbol of Christ). Liquid material placed in the pelican vessel would, when heated, vaporize, rising up into the small curved portion of the vessel where it would cool, condense and reenter the place it began as again a liquid. This imaged the alchemical operation of *circulatio,* a continuous circulation from one form of the substance to another that was thought to cause a subtle transformation in the material circulated.

From a modern chemical point of view, nothing would happen in such a process. But the image has profound psychological meaning, for it is a common experience in analysis that nothing seems to be happening for extended periods of time. Indeed, nothing may be changing on the conscious surface, but it is just at these times that the unconscious is often preparing a profound change. These preparations can often be seen in dreams during the period of apparent stagnation.

Another archetypal image for the boundary conditions of analysis is the *temenos,* which in the ancient world referred to a sacred boundary around a temple. In Roman times, it might be a furrow plowed around the site of a temple that was to be constructed. Even earlier, in ancient Egypt, the first action in constructing a new temple was for the Pharoah to "set the bounds" of the temple, marking off the sacred space of the temple enclosure. When Akhenaten, the "heretic" monotheistic pharoah of the Eighteenth Dynasty in old Egypt, set up a new capital city at Amarna, he had stones erected at the corners of the new site, each pillar saying that Akhenaten had caused the stone to be set as a boundary of his new sacred capital city. In modern times, the marriage custom of carrying a bride over the threshold of her new home is a mark of the special boundary, or *temenos,* of that now-special place.

Boundary conditions are more than mere agreements. They have psychotherapeutic utility in permitting a wide range of interpretation both within them and about them. Within the boundary conditions is a space marked off from ordinary life, a safe place where it is possible to reveal oneself in a way that would be inappropriate or unsafe in ordinary situations. It is a space in which one can experience the observant and helpful, but neutral, attitude of the analyst without having to concern oneself with the analyst as a person, except for the boundary conditions. Clearly, the person of the analyst remains present, and is part of the interaction, but in a manner different from persons outside the *temenos* of the analysis.

The boundary conditions should as far as possible be established at the beginning of therapy; they must be acceptable to both analyst and analysand and should not be altered by either party without mutual discussion. Thus both analyst and analysand have equal but different responsibilities in conducting the analysis. These are discussed below.

Responsibilities of the Analyst

A primary responsibility of the analyst is maintenance of the boundary conditions jointly (though not always explicitly) established with the analysand: being present at the appointed hour, not altering appointments or fees capriciously, giving the patient primary attention during the session, and focusing on the patient the skill and understanding that the analyst has acquired during training and practice. The analyst is as far as possible to be nonjudgmental and objective, in order to allow the analysand to verbalize thoughts about himself that he might otherwise be ashamed to confess.

The analyst does not expect that the patient will behave toward the analyst as toward a person in the social world, *except in the maintenance of the boundary conditions*. This means, in particular, that the patient can be angry and critical of the analyst without fear of retaliation, again respecting the boundary conditions, which are the mutually agreed, adult part of the interaction. Nor is the patient expected to socialize with the analyst.

Sexual Feelings: Bounded Intimacy

Sexual acting out between therapist and patient is a serious breach of the analytical contract, raising legal, ethical and moral questions. The occurrence of sexual *feelings*, however, is not unusual or surprising, since the bounded intimacy within the analytical *temenos* easily makes visible the most desirable aspects of persons as well as their flaws. The analyst is permitted to see the sometimes heroic struggles that occur in the personality of the analysand, unseen by the outside world. At times the patient also may appear dependent and vulnerable, which may evoke excessive care-taking, or even be sexually exciting to the analyst. It is the analyst's responsibility not to take advantage of the intimate atmosphere created within the *temenos*.

There is currently a great deal of interest in reported deviations from the professional prohibition of sexual interaction between analyst and analysand. Often the concern is expressed with polemical, sexist or feminist overtones. Since there are more male therapists than female therapists, there are inevitably more reported instances of sexual involvement between male therapists and female patients, which has tended to suggest a masculine mistreatment of women.

In my own experience over twenty-five years of practice, however, there have been only four cases in which a therapist has told me directly of involvement with a patient, so that the information was not hearsay. These four instances are evenly divided: two male therapists involved with female patients, and two female therapists involved with male patients. Whatever the popular perception may be, this is clearly a problem that involves therapists of both sexes. Further, in my experience of more than twelve years of combined service on the ethics committees of three professional societies, only one case of such sexual misconduct came to our attention, so it may not be as common as the sensational press would suggest.

In the four cases in which the analyst involved (and in two of the cases, the analysand as well) told me directly of the situation, the long-range outcome was quite mixed. One led to an enduring and successful marriage between analyst and analysand, one was disastrous for both parties, and in the other two situations the sexual acting out seems to have had relatively little long-range effect on either party.

While sexual involvement between therapist and patient is neither ethically nor legally permissible, and rightly so, the deeper psychological meaning of such lapses should be explored on an individual basis. Such exploration will help educate both therapists and patients to the dangers of acting on sexual feelings that often arise in the course of psythotherapy.

Some of the most destructive situations that have come to my attention have not been direct patient-therapist sex, but constellations in which a wife has become sexually involved with her husband's male therapist, obviously recreating an overcharged version of classical oedipal psychodynamics that in the several cases known to me were never completely resolved.

Sexual fantasies, unlike the literal acting out of sexual feelings, are a natural part of the analytical relationship, often appearing in dreams rather than in waking consciousness. These feelings can become a valuable part of the analysis if handled symbolically.[43] They often represent a deep psychological connection between the two persons, partaking of the archetypal imagery of the alchemical *coniunctio,* the union of opposites. They may foreshadow marked improvements in the psyche of the patient. Hence a patient's sexual feelings or dreams of the analyst should as quickly as possible be made a part of the analytical discussion, so their symbolic meaning can be explored. If the analyst has sexual feelings or dreams of the patient, however, they should only rarely be discussed in the analysis, lest they become a burden to the patient; they should of course always be part of the analyst's self-reflection in regard to the analysis, since they may represent an unstable part of the analyst's own personality.

Analytic Parameters and Therapeutic Skill

As already noted, the analyst is to bring to the analytic situation the therapeutic skill and experience of his or her particular style of doing analysis. Since the interaction of two people talking alone in a room closely resembles a social situation, the patient may at times be surprised when the analyst does not respond in an expected social manner.

For example, the analyst may choose not to answer questions about his or her personal life, such as marriage, children, church affiliation, etc. These ordinary categories of social discourse, if indulged in, tend to make the analyst "just another person," and diminish the possibility of the patient projecting important unconscious material onto the analyst—which is one of the ways of becoming conscious of the unconscious.

The projection of unconscious material by the patient onto the analyst is called *transference,* while the reverse process, where the analyst has unconscious expectations or distorted impressions of the patient, is called *countertransference.* Since both processes inevitably occur to some degree in any analytic situation, it is convenient to refer to them together with the abbreviation T/CT, standing for "transference and countertransference." They constitute much of the *transformative field* of the analysis within which many changes may take place in the analysand, and often also in the analyst. This is discussed more fully below.

The person beginning analysis may, after a time, want the analyst to "do the talking." Sometimes a patient is reluctant to speak of something because it has been previously discussed—"I've already told you that!" Such remarks are often based on a gross misconception of analysis—that it is a logical, problem-solving situation in which a certain amount of information is put into the analyst's mind and then answers come back. Of course, analysis does not work that way, and indeed the desired "answers" are more likely to come through the analysand's repeated attention to what is going on inside.

Actually, the transformation processes that go on in analysis have more to do with the unconscious structure of the mind than with anything that can be identified as a conscious, logical analysis of problems. The same difficulty must be dealt with repeatedly as long as it is a primary focus of feeling or affect. That is, it should be talked about without regard to repetition as long as it carries an emotional charge. This will be discussed more fully in chapter 6, on dreams and enactment techniques, where the evocation of affect-ego states is seen as a natural process in many dreams.

Protecting the Analysand

The analyst also has a responsibility to inform the patient when more rigorous treatment, such as hospitalization, might be necessary. Most Jungian analysts work largely with neurotic patients who seldom require hospitalization. But there are some situations, such as severe suicide impulses, where the patient should be told for his or her own protection that hospitalization is indicated. Or perhaps the less restrictive ego-support of medication might be sufficient. In extreme cases, the analyst has a legally mandated duty to notify a responsible member of the patient's family if the patient is clearly a danger to himself or to others. A legal commitment process may need to be instituted by the patient's family.

Such situations are rare, but any analyst should be prepared to deal with them if they arise. Where the analyst is not medically qualified, back-up contingency arrangements should be made with someone who is. Most depression is self-limiting, running out its course even if no medication or treatment is given. But medication and psychotherapy can considerably shorten the duration of depression, and, if understanding is acquired, decrease the likelihood of future recurrences. The overwhelming danger in severe depression is suicide, which I feel is always tragic—taking one's life because of a curable disease.

Responsibilities of the Analysand

Very little is written about the responsibilities of the analysand to the analyst, compared to the concern with the ethical and legal responsibilities of the analyst.[44]

The analysand has, of course, the obvious responsibility to make appointments on time and pay the bill promptly. The analysand also has a responsibility to work diligently on the analysis, which means giving close and constant attention to one's material. This will include recording dreams and personal associations to the dream images, and sometimes producing drawings, paintings or objects in clay or some other medium.

"Work" in this sense is not equivalent to "trying hard." Analytical work, for both parties, requires disciplined concentration and the development of specific skills such as "free-floating attention," where consciousness plays with various possibilities; this allows unconscious material to come up for conscious examination more than does "trying hard," which may even inhibit access to the unconscious. Above all, the analysand has an obligation to reveal emotionally important material, and to volunteer such information as soon as possible, thus minimizing the tendency to shrink away from dealing with central issues.

Some material can only be gathered by the analysand, such as dream notes, memories of the past and personal associations. While no patient can be faulted for not remembering dreams, they are rightly chided for not making every effort to remember them, for instance by putting writing or verbal recording materials close at hand when going to sleep. The patient has no responsibility to respect ordinary forms of social interaction with the analyst *within the temenos of the analysis.* Outside that *temenos,* however, the patient has the same responsibilities as the analyst, such as not divulging analytic material—including the analyst's remarks and interpretations—without permission of the other. Just as the analysand would expect the analyst not to make casual or judgmental remarks to others about the analysand, so should the analyst be shown the same respect by the patient.

Analysts do not gossip about patients and, conversely, patients should not gossip about analysts. In situations where many analysands know each other (not infrequent in many communities), a casual remark by one patient about a mutual therapist may seem to convey secret knowledge about the analyst and can interfere with the therapy of the person to whom the remark is made. Transference and countertransference feelings belong within the *temenos* of the analysis, where they can generate powerful understanding. If dissipated outside the *temenos,* the whole structure and outcome of the analysis can suffer. Confidentiality is the responsibility of *both* analyst and analysand.

The Transformative Field

Jung used a simple diagram to illustrate the psychological dynamics of relationships, with particular reference to the analytic situation.[45] As mentioned above, transference and countertransference (T/CT), the more or less unconscious perceptual distortions by, respectively, the analysand and the analyst, are a shorthand way of referring to the psychological interactions that make up the transformative field.

In addition to the conscious relationship between analyst and analysand, on which level the therapeutic contract establishes the boundary conditions, there is the relationship of each person to his or her contrasexual side. The analyst, if male, is related to his anima while interacting with the patient; the patient, if female, is related to her animus as well as to the analyst. Furthermore, the anima and the animus also interact directly, largely on an unconscious level. Thus Jung remarked that in any conversation between a man and a woman there are at least four persons involved. These relationships, which may be confusing when first encountered, can be shown in diagrammatic form (opposite).

In this model of the therapeutic relationship, which Jung based on a series of alchemical illustrations,[46] there appears to be an absolute symmetry between analyst and patient. This is misleading, because the diagram is basically meant to illustrate the equality between the male alchemist and his female co-worker, his *soror mystica* (mystical sister). When applied to the T/CT transformative

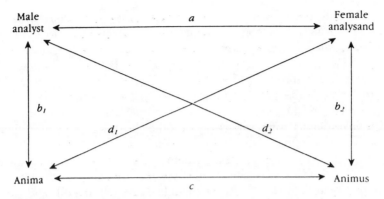

The transformative field: a = the conscious relationship; b_1 = the analyst's relationship with his unconscious; b_2 = the analysand's relationship with her unconscious, a principal focus of the work of analysis; c = the unconscious relationship between the anima of the analyst and the animus of the female analysand; d_1 = the animus of the analysand in relation to the conscious ego of the analyst; d_2 = the anima of the analyst in relation to the conscious ego of the analysand.

field, it requires two modifications: 1) the boundary conditions, once agreed upon, become more the responsibility of the analyst's conscious ego, and 2) the analyst assumes a larger responsibility for dealing with the activity of his or her own unconscious, so as to create a free and protected space in which the analysand can safely experience unconscious material that is repressed in ordinary life situations.

Transference phenomena are not something that a person beginning analysis should worry about. Falling in love with the analyst is not common. The distortions of transference are often subtle, or visible only in dreams. Transference may be positive or negative. One of the real dangers of negative transference is that early in analysis the patient may feel that the analyst is not supportive enough, and may even want to break off the therapy. The perception of the analyst as nonsupportive is often a projection of the patient's own self-rejecting tendencies, and is a proper subject for analysis. In fact, an analyst who is seen as especially supportive may be more difficult to share sensitive material with than one who is perceived to be decidedly neutral.

Although in most cases some transference develops in the course of the analysis, it would be a mistake to think that it takes a fixed amount of time to become evident. Some persons come to analysis with a transference already active before they walk through the door. This is particularly true if the analyst is already known by reputation, or through public lectures. The reverse situation might also be true—the patient being known to the analyst before their first meeting. In either case, both parties should be prepared to forego previous impressions of the other in order to remain open for the exploration of the analysand's mind.

One of my own most striking demonstrations of this need for a neutral attitude was when a high school friend came to me for professional help. I had always thought I knew him well, and considered him to be one of the few people who lived life in a natural, happy way, without undue concern for the opinions of others. This superficial impression of mine changed in the first few minutes of our professional interview as he told me in moving terms about his long depression. In another notable experience, a former teacher from my junior high school came as a patient. As an adolescent I had looked up to and admired him, never imagining that he carried the problems he revealed in my consulting room. Over an extended period of analysis, I came to admire him in a deeper way—for the courage he displayed in being honest with himself about his feelings and his shortcomings.

The field defined by T/CT may well be called transformative, for it is invariably true that the analyst will be transformed along with the analysand. In fact, one of the potent unconscious motivations for becoming a Jungian analyst is that one instinctively knows that one's psyche requires an immense amount of work, perhaps more than could be undertaken in even an extended Jungian analysis. The transformative field of the T/CT immerses the analyst in a continually enriched stream of personal experiences with analysands, activating material in the analyst that demands constant and disciplined psychological attention.

There is a repetitive mythological image, as expressed for example in the story of Chiron (the centaur, teacher of Asclepius), that to be a healer one must first oneself experience being wounded—that is, have first-hand knowledge of what it is like to be suffering and in search of healing. It follows that the healing of others' wounds has a reciprocal therapeutic effect on one's own painful lesions. Since neurotic pain is so common, there is little possibility of the analysand finding an analyst who has not personally experienced psychological wounding. Indeed, it is arguable that those who have not been brought to their knees by their own psychology are not good candidates for training as analysts.

A patient once dreamed that his likeness was being gradually carved from a glacial mountain of ice by flaming arrows shot by his lover. This slow, gradual emergence of one's own likeness also describes the subtle but inevitable reflexive effect upon the analyst of the multiple analyses in which he or she participates. We are all human and the transformative field of the T/CT is but a specialized form of the mutually transformative effect of any human interaction, an effect most vividly represented in the archetypal image of the *coniunctio,* the alchemical marriage.

If the analyst were entirely removed from proximity to the patient's world, in a safe and secure transcendent place, no effective analysis could occur. And if the analyst were too close to the patient, if the strength of the transference-countertransference were too great, the loss of boundaries would bring analysis to a stop. At a certain indefinable range, the relationship between analyst and analysand is a truly transformative field for both participants. Because this range is indefinable and shifting, analysis remains both a science *and* an art, just as Jung described it—a personal relationship within an impersonal professional framework.[47]

The Therapeutic Ratio

Jung is so often and superficially dismissed as a "mystic," particularly by biologically oriented therapists, that it is surprising to many to learn that when the International Congress of Psychiatry met in Zurich during the latter years of Jung's life, he was chosen as honorary president of the section discussing the possible biological basis of schizophrenia. This was in recognition of Jung's theory that schizophrenia (the term was coined by Jung's teacher, Eugene Bleuler) was the result of an as yet undiscovered "toxin X."[48] Jung was thoroughly scientific in his approach, but he chose to address himself to a wider range of natural phenomena than did orthodox materialistic science.

In discussing schizophrenia, Jung suggested two broad categories: 1) the situation where a normal conscious structure is overwhelmed by excessive pressure from the unconscious, and 2) the contrasting situation in which an ordinary amount of pressure from the unconscious would overwhelm an ego structure that was excessively weak.[49] This allows for the discussion of schizophrenia, and by implication neurosis and lesser psychological disorders, in terms of a therapeutic ratio.

If the ego is of average strength and the unconscious not excessively activated, a reasonable level of psychological health would be the result. The ratio of ego-strength to pressure from the unconscious would be greater than one. If the opposite were the case, with the unconscious pressure greater than the ego-strength, the ratio would be less than one; some form of mental disorder would result, ranging from mild anxiety through neurosis to severe mental illness.

An increase in the numerator (ego-strength) increases the therapeutic ratio. This can come about through ordinary supportive psychotherapy, or more frequent analytical sessions, or, perhaps the most extreme external support, hospitalization. The denominator of the therapeutic ratio can be decreased, again altering the balance toward stability (ratio greater than one), by decreasing the unconscious pressure. This can sometimes be done through psychotherapy that leads to either insight or a willingness to tolerate anxiety or depression. The pressure from the unconscious can also be effectively reduced through the use of medication, which should be used for only the shortest time necessary.

Medication

An understanding of the therapeutic ratio, as derived above from Jung's model of schizophrenia, permits a rational approach to the use of medication in Jungian analysis. Some Jungians have taken the extreme position that medication should never be used in analysis, that medication interferes with the patient "going through" the illness to achieve the understanding hidden in the symptomatic picture. I do not believe this antimedication extreme is correct, workable or humane. Medication can be a great help to the progress of Jungian analysis when it is judiciously and skillfully used.

There is a normal range of alertness, which if exaggerated may become anxiety. Conversely, too little alertness produces lethargy. At the midrange of alertness—more than lethargy and less than anxiety—useful analytic work can take place. If excessive anxiety causes the analysand to be above the useful range of alertness, mild use of tranquilizing medication may return functioning to the normal range, thereby permitting analysis to proceed. The same logic applies to excessive depression, which through careful medication can also often be returned to the midrange to facilitate useful and productive psychological work. There is even less reason to question the use of antipsychotic drugs when needed.

Jungian analysts who are also physicians vary in their use of medication concurrently with analysis. I myself use very little medication, perhaps in ten percent of my practice. Analysts who are not physicians often work closely with a physician or a physician-analyst when medication is needed. Anything that can help can also hurt. The analysand must take responsibility for using medication exactly as prescribed, so as to minimize the danger of unwanted side effects.

Leonardo's knot, made up of a single thread, is a contemplative meander which when unraveled leads to the heart of our nature. (*Concatenation,* School of Leonardo da Vinci, engraving, Italy, *c.* 1510)

5

The Process of Analysis

The actual course of analysis is difficult to describe. Like the individuation process itself, it may resemble a meander, that intricate decorative motif that suggests the unexpected and unpredictable turnings of a labyrinth. The course of analysis, like the course of life itself, is continually changing, according to the unpredictable emergence of new and novel ways of being.

This openness to new and creative possibilities is the essence of analysis. It can also be frightening for a neurotic ego, while professing to want the freedom to be itself, actually to find that freedom in the protected space of the analysis. No demand is made by the analyst that one behave in a certain way. One is free to talk of the present or the past, the inner world or the world of everyday life. What *is* frightening to many analysands is that this freedom will reveal them as they are, without their accustomed protective but imprisoning illusions about themselves or others.

In most cases, as mentioned earlier, this is shadow-anxiety, fear that the shadow, that "dark" side dimly known to the ego, will suddenly be revealed as the core of the personality. This cannot actually happen, for the contents of the shadow are simply aspects of oneself that could have been lodged in the ego or the persona, but were relegated to the shadow because they were unacceptable to the ego, in its own judgment, at the time the shadow-impulses arose. Integration of the shadow, which means reclaiming aspects of oneself that were "lost," inevitably enriches the ego.

A man in group psychotherapy, married and with maturing children, was terrified to admit to the group that he was having sexual feelings for one of the women in the group. As soon as he confessed the "terrible" truth, he blushed beet-red, buried his face in his hands and curled up in his chair, expecting massive disapproval from the other members of the group. In contrast, the woman for whom he had the sexual feelings was simply pleased that he found her desirable, while the other members of the group considered his feelings perfectly normal.

As he gradually uncovered his face and dealt with the actual reactions of the group, rather than burying himself in his fantasies of their disapproval, he was able to modify to some degree his excessive and primitive negative judgment of himself. His negative self-judgment for having normal sexual feelings was connected in his mind to his punitive and moralistic father, although even his experience of his father was different from the experience of his brother; the brother had rebelled against the father in adolescence, while this man in group therapy had remained subservient to his image of the father.

The unpredictable process of analysis is troublesome to the logic of the conscious mind, which would prefer that the difficulties of the personality could be approached as a problem to be solved. The expectation that the deeply unconscious growth process of the psyche can be managed with the attitude of an auto mechanic is simply a common misconception of analysis. The psyche is a living organism and interaction with it is like having a dialogue with another personality, one that may even speak another language. It is a further complication in analysis if the patient becomes self-critical about not being able to immediately understand and correct problem areas when they are identified.

Influencing one's own psychological processes is indeed of the order of complexity of learning another language. Tentative understandings, mispronunciations and embarrassing slips are to be expected. Being overly critical of oneself is a basic component of neurosis. But revelation of this attitude makes it accessible to the transformative field of analysis and is actually a cause for rejoicing, not depression.

The First Step: Self-Examination

The process of analysis proceeds by the simple expedient of examining as honestly as possible the material that arises from the patient's everyday life, past history, dreams and the T/CT interaction with the analyst. Underlying the entire process is the continual pressure of the archetypal Self to move the ego through the process of individuation. The boundary conditions of the analysis effectively insulate this exploration from immediate repercussions in the everyday world.

One behaves somewhat as an anthropologist of oneself when in analysis, entertaining novel theories as to the meaning of one's own behavior. Analytical self-observation, even with the help of the analyst, requires both moral courage and perceptiveness, essential ingredients of working successfully in analysis.

The Second Step: Compassion Toward Oneself

The neutral "anthropological" observation of oneself avoids the immediate excessive self-criticism that is a central component of the neurotic attitude. But self-criticism is by no means to be avoided, it is simply to be matured. Primitive self-criticism is harsh and judgmental, dividing the world into good and bad persons (with one's secret self usually one of the bad persons). An excessively rigid demarcation between ego and shadow is a result of such severe self-criticism.

The antidote to severe neurotic self-criticism is a compassionate attitude toward oneself. Although seemingly the most natural thing in the world, this is extremely difficult for many neurotic persons. It is sometimes an aid to compassionate regard for oneself to imagine oneself as the age at which a particular difficulty began. If a dream, for example, shows the dream-ego as a five-year-old child suffering a frightening situation, this may be a symbolic statement of a difficulty that arose in the mind about the age of five. Discussion on that period of life may clarify a situation that was traumatic for the patient at that time. It may then be useful for one to imagine oneself at that age, feeling the compassion that would naturally emerge in comforting a frightened child in the present.

If neurotic people actually followed the biblical injunction to "love your neighbor as yourself," they would be intolerable, for they would treat their neighbors with the same severe self-criticism that they internally inflict on themselves (and too often upon those who are emotionally close to them).

Stages of the Analytic Process

Any statement as to stages of the analytic process must be made with the clear understanding that, like the meander or the labyrinth, the process is not linear but convoluted. As with individuation, there may be general statements that are statistically true of a mass of people, but any statistical description is only a statement of probability; it is possible that no individual person exactly corresponds to the statistical norm.

It is nevertheless possible to speak of *likely* stages in the analytical process, even if in practice, for any particular person in analysis, they might occur in a different order. These can be described as the stages of analysis and synthesis.

The Analytic Stage

In the early period of analysis, the primary work is the establishment of the boundary, the analytical *temenos,* in which the analysis is to take place. This involves mutual agreement between patient and analyst on the contractual terms of their work, establishing schedules for meetings, etc. From a structural point of view, it is the stage of *working through the persona.* The patient must be willing to reveal himself to the analyst as he actually believes himself to be, at least to a greater degree than in ordinary relationships. This must be achieved without expecting a reciprocal revelation by the analyst, for it is the analyst's professional reserve that to a large extent creates the free and protected space in which the persona-mask can be dropped and the psyche of the patient can safely unfold. With uncritical acceptance from the analyst, it becomes clear that the rejection one fears from others is really self-rejection that is usually projected outward onto the world.

The part of the persona that is within the conscious control of the patient can be easily dropped. It is not unusual for a new patient, during the first interview, to reveal dark secrets that have never been told to anyone. Sometimes these are touching in their content—such as stealing something small from a store in childhood—but they may be as serious as having a child by someone else without the spouse's knowledge.

It gradually becomes clear that the deeper coloring of the persona cannot easily be dropped, even at will. The patient will know something that is important for the analysis but will withhold it, perhaps for months. Thus the patient becomes aware of internal resistance to analysis, in spite of the free and open space within the *temenos* of the analytic boundaries. When resistances are met, they reveal nodal points where there is a crisis of self-image. It is not the criticism of the analyst that is truly feared, nor the other members of the group in group psychotherapy, rather it is again the severe internal self-judgment. *To realize this is to come face to face with oneself as the real problem.*

The reluctance to permit the analyst to see behind the persona may come from a sense that one might be unable to regain the persona outside the analysis, where in many situations it would be appropriate or even essential. This is a groundless fear. A person who is able to drop the persona when it is *not* appropriate does not lose the ability to use it when it *is* appropriate. In fact, the ability to wear the persona as it was meant to be worn—like a suit of clothes that dresses one appropriately for the occasion without hiding the true person—is a valuable achievement and a mark of a successful analysis. Even when the analysand has achieved the ability to drop the persona during analysis, the same ability must be integrated in situations outside analysis, for instance in close relationships (though not in all social situations or relationships).

Following the stage of persona permeability in analysis, the next task is *identification and integration of the shadow.* This follows naturally, for the shadow is part of what is revealed behind the persona. In fact, the existence of a shadow is one reason for the elaboration of a persona. The persona and the shadow arise together in childhood, the result of sorting out acceptable and unacceptable behavior in relation to what the child really wants or is willing to relinquish.

The shadow is generally easy to identify. One simply looks at the nearest person of the same sex who has characteristics that one really does not like or disapproves of strongly. Because much of it can potentially be integrated into the ego, the shadow in dreams and fantasy material usually carries the same sex assignment as the ego.

The perennial surprise in getting to know one's shadow is that it is not all undesirable. Virtually without exception, the shadow contains some qualities that are needed for the further growth of the personality. Normal assertiveness is commonly repressed into the shadow, as is the ability to express affection freely—if that was experienced as undesirable or dangerous in childhood. There are some aspects of the shadow, of course, which still will be found unacceptable by the adult mind of the analysand (though these typically become fewer over the course of analysis). There are also

archetypal levels of the shadow that are not capable of integration
without severe disruption of the ego, but those do not arise in the
ordinary course of analytical treatment of neurotic problems.

Both the persona and the shadow can be considered in large part
as extensions of the ego, and can be integrated to a significant
degree. But the next layer of the psyche, the anima in a man and
the animus in a woman, is rather more difficult to grasp. Like the
persona, they are relational structures, relating the personal sphere
of the ego to the deeper layers of the objective psyche (collective
unconscious) or, if projected outwardly, relating the ego to aspects
of the world of collective consciousness. *Integration of the anima
or the animus* is an important and difficult step, largely because
they are most often experienced in projected form. Falling in love
or being fascinated with a person, usually of the opposite sex, is
often the first evidence of projection of the animus or anima. The
person on whom the anima or animus is projected may be the
analyst, but not necessarily so.

The anima or animus in a nonprojected form is relatively easy to
spot in dream material, and this is one of the most efficient ways
to gain a perception of these soul figures. The anima and animus
are particularly active in interpersonal situations, but that is also
one of the most difficult places for them to be perceived. Also, both
anima and animus can occur in positive or negative forms. In their
natural and positive form they facilitate connection outside the personal sphere of the ego. In their negative, neurotic form, however,
they become the coordinators of neurotic defenses that protect the
ego from danger while simultaneously excluding the ego from
growth, relationship and love.

Jung himself experienced the anima through difficulties in integrating his feeling function. Early in life, he had active imagination
conversations with his personified anima in order to get in touch
with his inferior feeling. Later in his life, von Franz once told me,
Jung did not need such imaginal interaction with the anima; what
the anima used to tell him in active imagination he now knew as a
direct sense of his own feelings and emotions. That is the natural
result of the successful integration of anima or animus.

Jung sometimes wrote as if the anima carried the inferior feeling
for all men (as it initially did for him), while the animus carried
women's inferior thinking. This was doubtless often true for those

raised in the traditional Swiss culture, who were the basis for Jung's observations in empirically formulating the concepts of anima and animus. In that markedly conservative society, men were indeed highly identified with their outer intellectual and social achievements, with little opportunity to develop their feeling, while women carried much of the feeling side of family and relationships, and had little opportunity to develop their thinking side in the outer world. But today, in a variety of very different cultural situations, one sees many anima and animus constellations that are vastly different from those described by Jung.

I have solved this theoretical dilemma, at least to my own satisfaction, by emphasizing the similar role of the anima or animus in enlarging the personal sphere of the ego's world. The specific *content* of the anima or animus depends upon what the culture, including the subculture of the original family system, emphasizes as masculine or feminine at that time and place.

One of my female patients once remarked that when she was in high school, if a girl wasn't a virgin she wouldn't admit it; but by the time she graduated from college, if a girl *was* a virgin she wouldn't admit it. The cultural mores had changed to such a degree that a healthy adaptation early in life could become maladaptive (in a collective sense, only) later in life. What was true for her in sexual standards is true in more subtle ways for many people in modern culture. Because individuation is the basic process and of such a personal nature, maladaptation to the social norm does not necessarily mean that the person is not on the correct path of individuation.

The hallmark of the negative and defensive form of the anima or animus is the nonpersonal, general nature of critical remarks made to others, usually to those with whom the person is emotionally close (since those further away may be simply dealt with through the polite persona). To hear the subtle shift into the anima or animus requires a trained ear, although many analysands, once they have recognized this in themselves, are able to sensitively identify it in others. Members in process group psychotherapy learn to help one another in becoming aware of this form of defensive interchange. This is also a major part of work with couples in marital therapy. Listening to a raw defensive interchange between the anima and the animus makes a dog and cat fight seem like time for high tea.

The Stage of Synthesis

By the time the analysand has identified and to some degree integrated the persona, the shadow and the anima or animus, much work has already been accomplished. The synthesis stage involves working through and integrating into everyday life the insights that have been discovered during the stage of intensive analytic probing. The process of integration may last much longer than the more diagnostic analytic phase, and shades imperceptibly into the use of the new insights in one's ordinary daily life.

What one discovers in most Jungian analytical situations is that one has been more highly influenced by unconscious assumptions and motivations than was realized. The unconscious processes are often of a defensive nature, designed to protect a dominant ego-image (which remember is *not* the same as the ego itself) from experiences that would threaten the maintenance of that image. One also comes to realize that the ego is not alone in the psyche, and is certainly not the master of the entire psyche but only the central reference point of consciousness—no little responsibility in itself!

Paradoxically, as the specific forms of the persona, shadow and anima or animus are identified and integrated, the ego becomes stronger, more comprehensive and simultaneously more humble. Beyond these figures of the persona sphere, both conscious and unconscious, lies the deeper realm of the collective unconscious, or *objective psyche*, which is the origin of the personal and also transcends it. The ego gradually learns that it is related to forces in the psyche which it can intuitively feel, or even respond to, but cannot grasp or control. At the center of the nonpersonal level of the psyche is the Self, the central archetype of order, which is the actual coordinating center of the psyche as a whole, expressing itself to the ego in many ways, including the making of dreams.

It is the Self that originates the *transcendent function*, which is Jung's term for the symbol-producing capacity of the psyche.[50] "Transcendent" in this sense does not mean transcendental (although the transcendental nature of the Self is a legitimate enquiry, particularly in the light of parapsychological phenomena). The transcendent function is the capacity to go beyond the tension of opposites through the creation of a symbolic form that transcends the level of the tension. Although this is a subtle process, it is not difficult to grasp in metaphor.

We have already discussed the tension of opposites, though not by that name, in terms of the recognition of shadow and persona and their partial integration by the ego. The shadow and the persona in themselves constitute a tension of opposites: the shadow is what the ego does not want to acknowledge, and the persona is what it may acknowledge even though it may doubt that it can actually live up to the image the persona presents to others. The ego is the final gate-keeper into action; it may try to guard the gateway, but with little success. What comes into one's mind is not necessarily one's "own" thought—it may come from another part of the psyche that is outside the integated part of the personal sphere. One is responsible for what one does, however, and it is the function of the ego to determine what action, if any, is to be taken.

But what does the ego do if there are opposing tendencies, both calling for realization in action? It is at this point that the ego is obliged to perform one of its most valuable and heroic analytic tasks—to hold the tension of opposites without putting either into action in the world. This is an extremely uncomfortable task for the ego, which is designed to interact naturally with the world. But it can be done. When the tension of opposites is successfully held, the psyche is stirred to manifest the transcendent function, permitting a symbolic solution where no logical solution was possible. Hence Jung called the transcendent function the *tertium non datur*, "the third not logically given." This symbolic solution often takes the form of a shift in the tacit structure of the ego identity, so that the tension of opposites no longer feels as acute. The tension is not solved, it is transcended in a more comprehensive vision.

A clinical example and an analogy may help to make this clear. The analogy consists of the forms in which water may occur—liquid, ice or steam, depending on the surrounding temperature. Ice and steam might be considered a pair of opposites, even though they consist of the same underlying substance, water. If ice and steam were opposites in a psychological sense, their integration would *not* be the room temperature water after the steam had melted the ice and both existed as liquid. That would be a too logical outcome for the unification of opposites. Rather, the integration of these opposites would be the *simultaneous* and compatible existence of the potentiality for "water" to exist as ice or as steam or both. The form of the water would vary in different situations, depending on what form was appropriate.

In a clinical psychological parallel, a patient might be trying to integrate the opposites of activity and passivity, or of aggression and affiliation. When the tension first comes to a focus in consciousness, there is often a resistance to change—"One can't *always* be assertive!" This is a remark by a woman who was too shy to call it to the salesperson's attention when she was not given the correct change! The integration of these opposites does not produce a midpoint between them—the lukewarm water—it produces an ability to express whichever opposite (or whatever mixture of them) is judged appropriate to one's true feelings and assessment of a particular situation at a particular time. The transcendent function produces a reintegration of these opposites into the ego in a different and more functional manner.

As the ability to deal with integration and synthesis of opposites progresses, the analysand often becomes aware (perhaps through dream imagery) of the relation of the ego to the Self. This is the sense of the center of the personality shifting away from the tensions of the ego trying desperately to cling to an image of itself, while the psyche opens to a more profound participation in the world and with others. There may then follow a stage of increasing awareness of one's particular destiny, along with the freedom to weave it in individual patterns.

Analysis Itself As a Stage

Life is not meant to be lived in endless analysis. Attention to one's unconscious is necessary in formal Jungian analysis, but diminishes as self-integration deepens. In this life one can never be rid of the problems of being human. After completing a successful analysis, subsequent developments later in life may again suggest a need to attend to the processes of the psyche, perhaps even resuming formal analytic sessions.

There is only one answer to how long one should stay in formal analysis: as long as it takes. In the next section I discuss ways to determine when to interrupt or end formal analysis.

Except in poetry or metaphor, it is difficult to describe the end-product of successful Jungian analysis. At the first Jungian congress that I attended, in Zurich, Edward Whitmont spoke of the end of successful analysis as *amor fati*, "love of one's fate"—being able to live with passion and depth in whatever historical situation one encounters. How different these images are from the image of the ego dominating its world, insensitive to the needs of others.

Speaking from the imagery of the East, Miyuki has presented the Zen ox-herding pictures from a Jungian perspective, offering one metaphorical image for the end of analysis.[51] After the ox (the natural mind) is tamed and ridden, it becomes so integrated that it "disappears"—which I understand to mean that it is so much a tacit part of the personality that it is no longer visible as a separate entity in the psyche. At such a point, the transformed person returns to society "with gift-bestowing hands," offering to others what has been obtained through one's own inner journey (see illustration on page 87).

The successful conclusion of Jungian analysis returns one to the world as a deeper and more integrated person, able to travel the road of individuation with only internal restraint and guidance, as needed, from the depths of one's own psyche. One is closer and more open to others, while simultaneously remaining more completely one's true self.

Beginning Analysis/Ending Analysis

It is always easier to determine when a person should enter analysis than when one should leave. If there is evidence of a neurotic interference with the progress of life, then analysis is indicated. Analysis may also be appropriate when one simply desires to look for deeper meaning and patterns in one's life.

The strongest motivation for going into analysis generally comes from the feeling that one is blocked or indeed absolutely at the end of one's tether. One is especially more able to endure the financial and emotional stress of analysis if one has previously tried other avenues to no avail. The feeling that "I can do it myself" dies hard, as does the tendency to intellectualize emotional problems that are simply not amenable to reasoning alone.

Some people who are attracted to Jungian analysis are afraid to begin for fear of it being an endless process. This comes from confusion between the process of self-examination, which *is* endless, and the process of formal Jungian analysis, which can be stopped or interrupted whenever the patient wishes (although this should not occur without discussing it first with the analyst).

Others hesitate to begin analysis for fear of becoming dependent on the analyst. This is a fantasy based upon an unconscious *wish* to be dependent. We all have such a wish, based on the positive experiences of childhood, but it is seldom strong enough to prove a difficulty in analysis. Although there may indeed be a period of some realistic dependence at the beginning, this generally dissipates as it becomes clear through analysis that it really is more enjoyable to be independent and have control of one's life. In truly adult life, episodes of limited dependency can actually be enjoyed without evoking the fantasy of overwhelming and irreversible neediness.

When the time has come to leave analysis, there may be some feelings of sadness in the analyst. When one has shared another's life so intimately, watching the other work through painful neurotic complexes, separation is bound to give rise to realistic feelings of loss. But when termination of analysis is appropriate, and agreed upon by both parties, the analyst's dominant feeling is more like the joyful pride of seeing one's child mature and leave home. That experience is also one of the real pleasures of being an analyst.

How Long Should Analysis Continue?

An analysis should continue as long as it is judged beneficial by both parties. This may be a short time, until the resolution of specific environmental and situational difficulties, or it may be for years.

Many people who have successfully completed Jungian analysis return at a future date to resume the process, for instance when significant problems arise at a new stage of life. Analysis is like lessons in the most difficult of all art forms—understanding oneself in depth. The art is never totally mastered, and review of oneself with another may always be of value.

When the analyst or analysand is considering ending the analysis, there are certain pitfalls to be avoided. If there is good faith on both sides, no great difficulty need be anticipated. The analyst or the analysand should introduce the topic for discussion, and a number of points should be kept in mind during the remaining sessions.

First, have the problems with which the analysis began been resolved or placed in an acceptable context? It is not necessary that they be "solved" in a usual sense, since many of life's problems cannot be solved as if they were puzzles. They may however be

Entering the City with Bliss-bestowing Hands, the last of the "Ten Ox-herding Pictures" of Zen Buddhism, represents the culmination of the process of individuation: "And now having moved through the stage of emptiness, and also having seen God in the world of nature, the individual can see God in the world of men. Enlightened mingling in the market place with 'wine-bibbers and butchers' (publicans and sinners), he recognizes the 'inner light' of 'Buddha-Nature' in everyone. He doesn't need to hold himself aloof nor to be weighted down by a sense of duty or responsibility, nor to follow a set of patterns of other holy men, nor to imitate the past. He is so in harmony with life that he is content to be inconspicuous, to be an instrument, not a leader. He simply does what seems to him natural. But though in the market place he seems to be an ordinary man, something happens to the people among whom he mingles. They too become part of the harmony of the universe."—Suzuki, *Manual of Zen Buddhism*.

seen in a healthier perspective, one that places them in a more acceptable and understandable context. The movement in analysis is often away from supposed outer problems to the realization that the problem arises within oneself. As the opossum Pogo, a now-deceased comic strip character said (in paraphrase of John Paul Jones), "We have met the enemy and we are they!"

Secondly, is there any evidence that some current problem area is being avoided? It may not be that an identified area that is well known to both analyst and analysand is being avoided; those areas are usually easy to see. Rather, it may be that a *developing* complex, one trying to surface in the analysis, is being avoided. Dreams are often the best clue to such a situation, hence it is well to look at a number of dreams after the question of termination has been raised. The unconscious itself may have something to say! After unilaterally deciding to terminate his analysis, one man dreamed that he was taking down a fence around his house, but he saw tigers across the street. (He elected to remain in analysis.)

Thirdly, is there any unexpressed emotional reaction toward the analyst, positive or negative in tone? Transference-countertransference (T/CT) forces can be strongly at work in the analysis and at times are not known to the analyst. There may be a negative reaction to something the analyst has said, or even something said by the analysand about the analyst outside the analysis. The unpleasantness of discussing negative feelings for the analyst must never stop one from bringing them into analysis. The results are always more likely to be positive than negative. It may be a situation, for example, where an unconscious complex of the analysand's is being projected upon the analyst and reacted to as if it were really a part of the analyst. This needs to be talked about, as does the parallel situation where the analysand feels that the analyst is unconsciously projecting.

Unacknowledged positive projections may also cause an analysand to propose a premature termination of the analysis. If the analysand is having strong sexual feelings for the analyst, for instance, they may be suppressed for fear of losing the analytical boundaries if the emotions are expressed. But analysts have generally experienced transference reactions to some degree in their own personal analysis, when they were in "the other chair," and are therefore not unprepared to deal with such feelings.

Consulting Another Therapist

When there is difficulty in the analysis, spoken or unspoken, the analysand may be tempted to consult another therapist without the knowledge of the personal analyst. To do this would be a breach of the analysand's responsibility to maintain and honor the boundaries of the analytic container. While one has every right to go to another therapist, it should not be done without first discussing the difficulty with one's present analyst. In any case, professional ethics require that the other therapist recommend returning to the present analyst to discuss the difficulties in person. The boundary conditions of the analysis are of primary importance and should be respected. They may be altered, but that should happen only after mutual discussion.

Following the medical model, a consultation with another therapist, a second opinion, is always allowed. The very personal quality of the analytic interaction, however, makes such consultation less useful than in medical situations, since the consultant cannot have as much tacit understanding of the situation as the primary analyst. Nevertheless, a session with an agreed-upon consultant may remove some instances of therapeutic impasse which might prematurely terminate an analysis.

The Natural Ending of Analysis

Since it is often not possible to tell if the analysis has come to a natural stopping point, one technique for determining this is to arrange for the analysis to stop for a period of time, say for three months, and then resume for an equal period of time. Alternatively, analytical hours can be scheduled at increasingly longer intervals. Both methods allow the analysand to experience an absence of the usual analytic schedule and may reveal strengths or problems that were uncertain in the context of regular sessions.

If the analysand is also in group psychotherapy and planning to discontinue that as well, notice of termination should be given to the group at least one month prior to termination. That allows the members of the group to also assess the patient's readiness to leave therapy. Groups often act as a sensitive indicator of the mental state of the person considering termination. Certain group members may need time to say their own goodbyes, or to express a sense of personal loss if the departing patient has been of special help.

When Jungian analysis ends with the agreement of analyst and analysand, with no indicators of hidden or unresolved complexes and with the option to resume analysis if indicated in the future, there is a sense of mutual achievement for both analyst and analysand. The primary achievement is always the analysand's, but the analyst too can take pleasure in what has been accomplished. Even at the time of a successful termination, it may not be possible to say with any finality what caused the analysis to be "successful." The unconscious personalities of both parties are continual participants in the process; much of the credit belongs to them as well.

When analysis ends naturally, the subsequent relationship between analyst and analysand generally takes the form of mutual respect. There are unlikely to be mutual projects and time-sharing in the future, such as analysis provided, but the feelings they have shared can last a long time.

6

Dreams and Techniques of Enactment

In all religions and in all early civilizations, dreams have been considered an important gateway between the everyday world and another world—the spirit world, the world of the gods, the archetypal realm—in modern language, the unconscious.

Dreams were important in both the Old and the New Testaments. Joseph was the outstanding dream-interpreter of the Old Testament, correctly interpreting the dreams of Pharoah, so that the land of Egypt could store grain during seven years of plenty, avoiding famine during the ensuing seven years of famine. In the New Testament, it was a dream that told Joseph to take Mary and the infant Jesus and flee to Egypt to avoid the slaughter of the innocent children ordered by Herod. It was also a dream that told him it was safe to return.

The Buddha's mother dreamed that a white elephant with seven pairs of tusks entered her side. This was interpreted to mean that she would give birth to a son who would be a savior of the whole world. In ancient Greece and Rome, the temples of Asclepius were healing shrines where the supplicant of the god slept ("incubated") in the temple precincts, hoping for a dream whose interpretation would both diagnose the cause of the illness and offer suggestions for cure. The *Oneirocritica* by Artemidorus of Ephesus, a dream manual from the early Christian era, clearly reflects a widespread interest in the meaning of dreams.[52]

Many historical persons have left records of their dreams: Julius Caesar, Descartes, Bismarck, Hitler, Freud and Jung, among many others. But by 1900, when Freud published his most famous work, *The Interpretation of Dreams*, there was virtually no scientific or professional interest in dream interpretation.

Freud's Dream Theory

Almost single-handedly, Freud created a new framework for the clinical understanding of dreams, which became an important activity in the new therapy of psychoanalysis. Dreams were called "the royal road to the unconscious."

In the classic Freudian view, the dream is a method for maintaining sleep in spite of unacceptable impulses—usually sexual or aggressive—that arise when the censorship of the conscious mind is relaxed during sleep. The unacceptable impulse which might disturb the sleeper is transformed into a more acceptable and dramatic form by the dream work, using such mechanisms as displacement and condensation. Displacement, for example, is unconsciously moving the repressed sexual wish for the mother to the dream image of a more acceptable substitute woman, thereby hiding the incestuous nature of the wish. In the mechanism of condensation, several discrete figures are condensed into one composite figure that stands for all of them. Secondary elaboration, such as disguising actual persons and events, is used to put the resulting images into more acceptable form before they are experienced as a dream. The dream in the Freudian view allows a partial discharge of the original impulse, without allowing it to appear in such a primitive form as to awaken the dreamer.

In Freudian dream interpretation, the free-association of ideas to the motifs of the dream is supposed to lead back to the original and undisguised latent dream behind the experienced and remembered manifest dream.

Jung's View of Dreams

Jung originally worked with the Freudian theory before breaking with Freud and developing his own vision of the nature of the unconscious mind. What is unique about Jung's view is that it avoids making the dream into a disguised conscious message. There is no latent or hidden dream in Jungian theory. Instead, the dream is a *symbolic* representation of the state of the psyche, showing the contents of the personal psyche (the complexes) in personified or representational form as persons, objects and situations that reflect the patterning of the mind.[53]

Contents from the deeper part of the psyche sometimes are seen in dreams. These are archetypal images and motifs that may not be recognized as such unless one is familiar with the symbolism in mythology and folklore. At times, the appearance of archetypal images in a dream indicates a profound change in the state of the psyche.[54]

Jung criticized Freud's theory for overlooking the fact that many dreams seem to mean exactly what they say. Considering the dream as a disguised version of what might be a waking thought seemed unnecessary for many dreams that were clear without interpretation.

Dreams may make jokes, solve problems or even deal with philosophical and religious issues. For Jung, dreams were a self-representation of the state of the psyche, presented in symbolic form. The purpose of dreams in Jungian theory is to compensate the one-sided distortions of the waking-ego; they are therefore in the service of the individuation process, helping the waking-ego to face itself more objectively and consciously.

When I was first in psychiatric practice, I attempted for more than two years to use both Freudian and Jungian theory in dealing with the dreams of patients. The result was that I became convinced of the superior clinical usefulness of the Jungian approach. This was a number of years before I entered training to become a Jungian analyst. I have subsequently devoted a great deal of attention to dream interpretation, including such specialized areas as the appearance of religious imagery in dreams.[55] Dream interpretation is in my opinion still the most direct road to an appreciation of the unconscious mind. The clinical use of dreams in Jungian practice is greater than in most other forms of psychotherapy or psychoanalysis because Jungians have an unusually strong training in recognizing and honoring the meaning of unconscious material such as dreams.

Although the manner in which dreams are analyzed naturally varies among Jungian analysts, there are some common practices followed by most in the analysis of dreams. The major points of Jungian dream interpretation will be discussed here one by one:

1. Remembering dreams—how to get the basic data of the dream.
2. Recording dreams so that they can be used most effectively in analysis.
3. Amplification of dreams through a) personal associations, b) cultural associations, c) archetypal associations and d) natural associations.
4. The dramatic structure of most dreams.
5. The purpose of dreams—compensation of the waking-ego's views.

Remembering Dreams

Modern research in the physiology of dreaming indicates that everyone dreams several times during every night of sleep. It is only under laboratory conditions that a person can be deprived of dreaming sleep. Even then, if allowed to sleep without interruption, much of the missed dream time is recovered.

Some people do not so readily remember their dreams upon awakening, often feeling that they do not dream at all. Dreaming occurs approximately every ninety minutes during sleep. The dream takes about the same amount of time as watching similar action on television. Dreaming is most often associated with light sleep (following deeper sleep) together with rapid eye movements (REMs), which some researchers think are following movements in the dream. It seems that the ninety-minute dream cycle also occurs during the day, but is covered over by the activity of the conscious mind.

For most people, dreams fade rapidly after waking up. This is true even if upon first awakening the dream seems so vivid that it could not possibly be forgotten. One is advised in Jungian analysis to keep a dream journal, recording a dream the moment it is remembered, even during the night. For this purpose, it is best to keep writing materials right at the bedside, making notes the moment the dream is recalled. Some people prefer to use a tape recorder rather than make notes, in which case it is often more efficient to transcribe the verbal report and bring the written notes to analysis. A written dream report can be handled more rapidly than having the analyst listen to a recorded dream.

Dreams may come back into memory during the first hour after awakening, or sometimes later in the day when an event may remind one of a motif in the dream. Notes should be made, if possible, the moment the dream is remembered.

Even if one "never dreams," it is still not unusual for dreams to be remembered after analysis has begun. Putting writing materials or a tape recorder by the bedside seems to stimulate dream recall. A simple technique for remembering dreams is to tell oneself when going to sleep, "I will dream and remember my dreams." Such self-suggestion acts somewhat like hypnosis to increase dream recall.

The Dream Record

The record of the dream should contain as much detail from the dream as possible. Because dreams are symbolic statements of deeper realities in the mind, even a small detail in a dream may be symbolically significant. Sometimes a person will report dreaming only of everyday events, with no symbolic meaning, but when the dream reports are actually examined some small variation from the everyday event will reveal a symbolic meaning. For instance, a person might dream of an office situation connected with stress, "just like it is," but the dream report indicates that it is snowing outside, whereas the actual time of the year is midsummer.

The dream report might also usefully contain the dreamer's personal associations to the motifs of the dream. Since these are unknown to the analyst, including them in the written dream report can speed the analytic interpretation of the dream. One way to include such associations is to put them in parentheses immediately after the motif. For example, a dream report might read: "I dreamed I was having dinner with Aunt Minnie (my father's older sister, who never married, whom I visited a lot when I was preschool, made delicious cornbread . . .)." Alternatively, the associations to persons and situations can be listed after the dream.

Amplification of Dreams

The three usual levels or types of amplification of dream motifs are personal associations, cultural associations and archetypal associations. A fourth type of association can also be used: what the motif in the dream is actually like. A tornado, for example, can be known to be dangerous without any personal, cultural or archetypal associations. I call this type of association a natural association. While both the dreamer and the analyst might contribute to cultural and archetypal associations, only the dreamer can supply the personal associations to the dream. The inclusion of archetypal associations is one of the unique characteristics of Jungian dream work.

Personal Associations

Personal associations consist of the dreamer's own immediate thoughts on the images in the dream. In the Jungian approach, one

stays close to the particular image, avoiding extended free-association (associations to the associations to the associations). Each
image or motif in the dream is treated as the best available symbol
at that time to represent a part of the psyche that is involved in the
dream. Since the dream image is seen as a representation or per-
sonification of a complex in the dreamer's mind, associations to the
image may reveal other aspects of the complex.

Personal associations are just those thoughts that come naturally
into the dreamer's waking mind when the dream image or motif is
considered. For example, a man dreamed that he was eating a plate
of cooked beaver tail and pieces of pineapple. There were no personal associations to beaver tail, except that he had read it was
considered a delicacy, and he knew the words "beaver" and "tail"
were both slang expressions for female genitalia. To the pineapple,
however, he associated a time earlier in his life when he asked why
there were so many pineapple motifs on hotels and homes in
Alexandria, Virginia. He was told that in the days of sailing vessels,
a ship captain returning with a load of pineapples would stick one
on his gate to let friends know that he was home. This personal
association to pineapple suggested that a particular time in the
patient's life might be relevant to the meaning of the dream.

Cultural Associations

At times a dream motif has an obvious cultural meaning, even
though that may not be spontaneously mentioned by the dreamer in
reporting the dream. An example would be the president of the
United States, or the queen of England—persons who through projection carry an important cultural meaning, even though we usually
take such meaning for granted. For instance, several of my patients
had dreams showing marked reactions to President Kennedy's
assassination, one experiencing a great upsurge of feeling about her
brother who had died in combat, one feeling a sense of the tragic
flaws in all mankind, another reacting with strong oedipal overtones. Each responded to the external event of Kennedy's death as
if it were immediately relevant to the internal structure of their own
minds.

When the analysand does not mention an obvious cultural
association, one may think of this omission as being caused by
unconscious defenses. Rarely, the analysand will even deny the
association when it is suggested by the analyst. The exploration of

such avoidance can often yield interesting psychodynamic insights.

Associations to movies, television programs, plays and novels, although seldom referred to in texts on dream interpretation, may be very useful when there is some motif in the dream that readily brings up the fictional material. For instance, a man recently dreamed of being in a room with "J.R.," the central character in the television drama *Dallas*. The character was meaningful to the dreamer's own psychology, and even more interesting was that he felt in his dream it was not "really" the character J.R., but the actor who played the part of that character. His associations to this motif were that the actor, Larry Hagman, the son of actress Mary Martin, was almost the opposite of the character J.R. he portrays in the television series. This cultural association raised many valuable questions about the current psychodynamics of the dreamer, including the relationship of his persona to his actual sense of himself.

Archetypal Associations

A specialized aspect of Jungian analysis, one which sets it apart from other approaches to depth psychology, is the concept of the archetype and the archetypal amplification of dream motifs. Archetypes in their pure form are the structuring patterns of the mind, without any specific content. One does not "inherit" an archetypal image, but one has an innate tendency to structure experience in certain ways; one's internal image of the mother, for example, is based upon the archetypal tendency to structure early experience so as to form a mother image.

While one can do very good psychotherapy, including dream interpretation, without the level of archetypal amplification, there are instances in which it adds a dimension, and opens vistas of understanding, that are not otherwise available. One of the most frightening dreams I ever had myself was of a cone of silvery metal growing in my right knee. In the dream, I was able to lift out the cone of metal and see the functioning of the inside of the knee. In the same dream, there were pieces of golden metal growing like discs in the calf of that leg. I could remove the discs, but they left indentations in my flesh. My immediate thought upon awakening from the dream was that something foreign, and clearly not part of the body, was growing in it. Perhaps I had cancer!

But when I took this dream to Marie-Louise von Franz, with whom I was in analysis at the time, she pulled the book *Origins of*

European Thought[56] from her shelf, turned to the chapter on "Birth from the Knee," and brilliantly amplified the dream on an archetypal level that totally overshadowed the cancer hypothesis. Then, in active imagination, I was able to carry the dream further, discovering an additional alchemical meaning to the "metal" growing in the body. The nature of the dream required archetypal amplification in order for me to understand the process of rebirth that was taking place in me at that time.

Archetypal amplifications are usually more readily supplied by the analyst, since the study of historically recurring symbols and motifs is a basic part of the training of Jungian analysts. But anyone thoroughly immersed in his or her own analysis will be moved quite naturally to amplify personal material in this way, for instance by broad reading in religion, mythology and fairy tales, as well as frequent reference to dictionaries of imagery.

No one can know all there is to know about archetypal images. Their meaning can never be exhausted and knowledge of such images is a continual study contributing to the art of analysis. But if overused, or introduced when the analysand has no way of integrating the information, archetypal amplification can become a sterile form of reductionism, substituting the archetypal meaning for the personal meaning to which the image is related. The use and misuse of archetypal interpretation is a subject of much ongoing discussion among Jungian analysts.

Natural Associations

Sometimes it is helpful to amplify images in dreams through natural associations, which are simply the way the dream motif would be known to function if it were part of the natural world. A maned lion, for example, may prompt few personal associations other than the zoo for someone who has lived in an urban culture. There may be cultural associations, such as the lion and unicorn on the British royal coat of arms. On an archetypal level, the lion has a vast range of meaning: "king of the beasts," the archetypal Self, the "Greene Lyon" of alchemy, the ancient Egyptian guardian of the gateways of dawn and dusk, and even the animal form of St. Mark, one of the four Apostles, in Christian iconography.

A natural amplification of a maned lion, however would simply include thoughts on how male lions are known to behave in their natural state. Among these would be that male lions are poor hunters compared to female lions, and tend to be seen as lazy, letting the female bring them a kill for dinner. They also are one of the rare animals that will mate when the female is not in rut, and in that manner they resemble mankind. These natural associations of a male maned lion are in contrast to the heroic image of vitality that one generally finds in archetypal amplifications.

Occasionally the various levels of amplification appear contradictory, and the most appropriate meaning of the dream image can be determined only intuitively in the context of the actual dream, or the series of dreams in which the image appears.

The Dramatic Structure of Dreams

Most dreams have a dramatic structure, with a beginning problem, complications and developments, and often a lysis or solution, followed by a result, a change in the original situation of the dream. Dreams are like personal dramas, staged by and for the dreamer to help the dream-ego move further in the process of individuation. The dramatic structure of dreams faces the ego with situations that are symbolically important. The actions or inactions of the dream-ego are particularly significant, frequently altering the course of the dream (or subsequent dreams in a series).

The dramatic structure of dreams may be a means of inducing affective states in the dream-ego, producing a dream form of the affect-ego that Jung noted in discussing the word-association experiments.[57] The affect-ego is a distortion of the usual ego state, due to the ego being influenced by one or more activated psychological complexes.

Clinical experience suggests that unless the ego is in contact with an active form of a complex, and suffering the affect thereby generated, it cannot really alter the structure of the complex, however much it "knows" in an intellectual manner about the complex. Alteration of a complex, then, requires the ability to endure the distortions of the affect-ego state associated with the complex, while at the same time not losing the sense of the affect being due to a complex rather than one's integrated functioning.

The dramatic structure of most dreams is ideally suited to experiencing affect-ego states, and thereby also offers the possibility of altering the complexes that generate those states. Like the analytical boundary, the dream produces a free and protected space because the dream-ego can always awaken into the everyday world, although during the dream it does not usually know it is in a dream state.

Not all dreams are dramatic in form. Some are simply one single image. Although most dreams are visual, there are dreams that are entirely auditory. Even in dreams that have the usual dramatic structure, it is possible to look at them as displaying the proximity of the complexes that are pictured in the dream. This is something like reading a dream backward.

For instance, one might dream of being in one's childhood home and trying to read a book, but the words make no sense. Looking at this dream in a static fashion, it would suggest that in the presence of the complex (the "childhood home") something interferes with "reading," the learning process. Looked at in reverse, it might indicate that the activity of "reading" is not to be trusted when in the vicinity of "childhood home."

Even dreams that are simple in structure can be seen to have a dramatic relationship, in terms of compensation, to the waking-ego. No dreams are purely static. The static view is actually an abstraction, a way of reading the dream as if it were an index to complexes and a gauge of their proximity, rather than in the service of compensation and individuation. Nevertheless, it can be a valuable clinical tool if used judiciously.

Compensation in Dreams

Compensation (in the sense of modification) of the distorted or incomplete views of the waking-ego is the purpose of dreams according to Jungian theory.[58] Our waking views are always incomplete, so there is always room for compensation. It is as if the dream were made by a larger, more superior personality, the "greater" version of ourselves, one somehow outside the fears and tensions of the waking-ego. Thus, the theoretical origin of the dream is the Self, the regulating center of the psyche. Far from the Freudian view of dreams as merely the guardian of sleep, the Jungian approach sees the dream as a part of the very texture of life, related to individuation and not simply to problem-solving of concern to the waking-ego.

Sometimes the attitude or viewpoint of the waking-ego requires little correction. In such instances, dreams may make only minor compensations, complementary to the viewpoint of the waking-ego. Rarely, the dream compensates not only the personal situation of the dreamer, but one's family situation. This is particularly true in some children's dreams, which are notorious for revealing active complexes in the parents.[59] If the waking-ego is engrossed in the search for the solution to a particular problem, the dream may give a symbolic clue to the answer. The most famous case in science is the dream of Kekule in which he solved the problem of how to arrange the carbon atoms in benzene; the dream showed a snake holding its tail (an image known in alchemy as the *uroborus*) and he suddenly realized that he could arrange the carbon units in a circular fashion—the benzene ring.

Understanding the compensatory nature of dreams requires that they be seen as in a dialectical relationship to the waking-ego. The dream does not tell one specifically what to do, rather it comments on the waking attitudes and opinions relevant to what one wishes to do. In order to make use of the compensating information in the dream, therefore, a conscious attitude must first be established.

If the conscious attitude is greatly exaggerated, the compensating comment of the dream may be likewise exaggerated but in the opposite direction. For instance, if a person consciously is very angry at another person and yet dreams that he or she is in love with that person, it would not follow that the dreamer is actually in love instead of angry; the dream's exaggeration in the opposite direction would more likely be aimed at achieving a balanced attitude in consciousness.

While it is not desirable to turn the direction of one's life over to dreams, they can be valuable aids in identifying and correcting unrecognized distortions and blind spots in consciousness.

The compensatory nature of dreaming is never simply a static balancing between the dominant conscious attitude and its opposite. Instead, compensation is finally in the service of wholeness—that is, the dream compensates the present form of the conscious ego-image in terms of the potential wholeness of the psyche, which is the underlying pressure toward individuation.

Dreams in Analysis

It is arguably possible to do a complete Jungian analysis when there are no dreams available, but that is rare and almost never necessary.

Dreams are invariably the source of valuable information for analytic work, not only because they are the most common manifestation of unconscious activity, but also because they provide a viewpoint that is demonstrably more objective than that of either the analyst or the analysand. Dream interpretation both speeds and deepens the analytical process.

Jungian analysts vary greatly in their style of using dreams in analysis. I prefer that analysands bring a written account of their dreams, with an extra copy for myself to incorporate into my case file. It is helpful if the dreams are dated and presented in sequence, with personal associations and daily events at least briefly noted in the dream report. This permits the analyst to scan a number of dreams, see them in the context of the dreamer's life, and focus upon those that seem most potentially valuable. Alternatively, the analyst might ask the analysand to pick one or two dreams that seem particularly significant.

Defensive Use of Dreams

Though dreams are valuable, patients can use them in a defensive fashion, as they can all other information. There are two ways of using dreams defensively that are rather easily recognized and avoided. The first is never to bring dreams to the analytic hour, especially when they seem to be revealing about oneself. The other is to bring so many dreams that they overshadow any other aspect of the analysis, such as the fierce quarrel with one's spouse the night before.

Dreams can be denied importance, even though they are brought to the analytic session. A frequent form of such denial is to attribute the dream only to actual events of the present: "I dreamed about the Rolls Royce because I saw one parked near my car yesterday." The flaw in that attitude is that one sees many things every day, but only a few appear in dreams. The dreams may indeed select from everyday events (what Freud called "day residue" of incompletely integrated perceptions)—but the *manner* in which the image from the day is incorporated into the dream is invariably unique and in keeping with the dramatic structure and intent of the dream. Residual images of the day, together with memory images, may constitute the stage props in the dramatic form of the dream, but they do not determine how they are used in the drama. A chair may be an incidental item to sit in, or it may appear as the defensive tool of a lion-tamer in the circus.

Enactment Techniques

The same unconscious structures of complexes that are imaged and personified in dreams can be worked with in other ways that utilize the unconscious. The projective hypothesis, upon which much psychological testing is based, is that an unstructured situation will be structured to a significant degree by the contents of the unconscious mind that are constellated at the time of testing.

The same general consideration underlies Jung's theory of psychological types—that a person possesses a relatively fixed way of approaching life, basically in an introverted or extraverted way, and that way will be most prominent in dealing with new and unstructured situations. The value of all enactment techniques lies in producing an image or form for the constellated unconscious activity. This form permits the waking-ego to take an attitude toward what before was merely unconscious, producing symptoms but not insight and understanding.

In the use of enactment techniques in Jungian analysis, an unstructured situation or material is provided. It may be clay or painting materials, with which the image from a dream (or significant symbol from elsewhere) is to be expressed. At the annual conference of the C.G. Jung Educational Center of Houston, there is always an opportunity for molding in clay, with the productions discussed psychologically and displayed at the end of the conference. Also, there is traditionally a section on writing poetry, another way of expressing unconscious contents. Dance therapy is a new and valuable tool for the same purpose; there are now several trained Jungian analysts who are also registered dance therapists. Another enactment technique widely used by Jungian analysts is the sandtray, in which imaginal scenes are constructed.

One technique that is little known but amazingly powerful, is having the patient write letters to a significant person, often a parent, even if that person is deceased. It then is often of additional value to have the analysand write a letter "back" from the person.[60] Sometimes several interchanges in such "letters" reveal an unusual amount of unconscious material, particularly feelings that have been dissociated from the images in consciousness to which they naturally belong.

Dramatic forms of enactment can be used in both individual analysis and in process group therapy. The gestalt "empty chair" technique, placing a significant person (or a version of oneself) in an empty chair and carrying on a dialogue, perhaps playing both roles and changing chairs, can in many instances bring forth both affect and information. Sometimes this gestalt technique is modified into a minor psychodrama, with the analyst or a member of the therapy group playing one or more of the roles.

Sandtray Projections

Both my wife and I studied the use of the sandtray with Dora Kalff when I was in training in Zurich. It has since become a favorite and fascinating enactment technique. New patients are asked to construct three pictures in the sandtray, which is a set size, selecting items from several hundred figures and forms that are available in the same room. Sometimes a topic is assigned for the sandtray, such as "your family of origin," or "your marriage," or even "your concept of God." At other times, the analysand is told to "pick out what objects catch your attention and make an arrangement of them in the sand." The sandtray is not restricted to new patients; analysands may request it to amplify a particular dream motif or complex area.

Self-developing, instant photographs are made of the sandtray, as well as process notes indicating which items are picked in what order, which discarded or changed, spontaneous comments, etc. At times the analyst may interact with the patient in terms of the sandtray, asking if certain figures can be repositioned or substituted. Items may be added to the sandtray picture, with enquiry as to the analysand's feeling about the addition. So the sandtray can be used to enact dream images or complexes, and it can also be constituted as a symbolic dialogue of the analysand with the completed picture, using reactions to alterations in the tray. It is amazing how a person sometimes will resist with great feeling a minor change in the sandtray picture. Such strong emotional constellations give one a sense of the reality of the psyche underlying the construction of the projective picture in the sandtray.

The same forms of amplification—personal, cultural, archetypal and natural—can be used for sandtray scenes as for dreams. The sandtray is now popular with a number of Jungian analysts, and interest in this technique seems to be rapidly spreading.

Hypnoanalysis

Some enactment techniques take place primarily within the psyche of the analysand. They are particularly suited to work with introverted persons who may dislike group work or feel inhibited about constructions in art therapy or in the sandtray projective technique.

Hypnoanalysis is one such internal enactment technique. Some Jungian analysts, professionally trained in the use of hypnosis, combine it with a classic approach to analysis. I have done a great deal of work with hypnosis,[61] but use it sparingly in my analytical practice, preferring dreams as a deeper revelation of the psyche than is possible in most uses of hypnoanalysis. Even deep hypnosis still involves some degree of ego involvement in the imagery, while dreams are as close to a pure sample of the unconscious as we are able to obtain.

If the analysand is a good hypnotic subject, the revivifications under hypnosis approach the affect-ego states of dreaming. They are used in the same manner, the analyst helping the patient to take an attitude toward the images in the hypnotic trance. Except in specialized situations, there is little attempt to direct the hypnotized patient as to what to experience in the trance state. Hypnoanalytic techniques are discussed more fully in the next chapter.

Active Imagination

Active imagination is a technique devised by Jung for direct interaction with the unconscious through a controlled imaginal state while one is awake. It is a form of meditation that in some ways resembles self-hypnosis. Active imagination, however, differs sharply from fantasy and day-dreaming by the incorporation of two fundamental rules:

1) The attitude of the ego (the "imaginal-ego") in active imagination must be the same as if the imagined situation were a real one. That is, the moral, ethical and personal rules that apply to a situation in waking life must be followed in the imaginal sequence as well. This prevents the psyche from splitting and elaborating fantasy images that "don't count" because they do not come into contact with the complexes that are troublesome to the waking-ego.

2) When situations or persons *other than the imaginal-ego* react to the ego in active imagination, they must be permitted to react *with no interference whatsoever from the ego*. This seemingly easy rule is very hard to follow, for it is tempting in active imagination to "fix" a difficult situation as one would in fantasy. One of my own realizations of this occurred when I had a difficult impasse with my analyst and went, in active imagination, to a wise old man

image who had always given good, practical advice. I asked him what to say to my analyst about our difficulty and he surprisingly said, "Don't say a word to her, just take this sword and kill her!"

That was a real dilemma, for to have acted as he advised would have gone against the first rule of active imagination—not to do something that one would not do if it were a real situation. And yet, the wise old man figure had *always* given me good advice. In desperation, I concluded that I would imagine starting after her with the sword "as if" I meant to kill her, although I would stop short of the deed. As I acted, in imagination, upon this decision, the figure of my analyst changed to an animal form that I could, though with reluctance, kill with the sword of the old wise man.

This active imagination sequence was the turning point in my whole analytical experience, for it destroyed my unconscious dependence upon the analyst. By the time of the next appointment it did not really matter to me what my analyst's position was, because now I had a deep sense of my own foundations. When I told her the active imagination, and my dilemma, she commented, "That animal form was my animus, you can kill that!" I was convinced forever of the value of active imagination.

There is a third, ancillary rule of active imagination, recommended by many analysts, that had given me cause to hesitate in the sequence described above. The rule is that *you should not do active imagination involving real people.* There are two reasons for this advice, one practical and one dealing with the theoretical nature of the unconscious. The practical reason is that if one does active imagination with a real person, it may give only a symbolic solution to the problems with that person, while short-circuiting interaction with the real person and inhibiting an actual solution in the everyday world. Active imagination, like analysis, should be an aid to living, not a substitute for life.

Because one does not know how the deep unconscious of one person interacts with that of another, and because there *are* synchronistic occurrences, doing active imagination involving a real person can also be seen as similar to the early ideas of sympathetic magic—where the shaman or medicine man would attempt to change a person through interaction with an image of that person. This reason for not involving living persons in one's active imagination will carry more or less weight depending upon one's metaphysical assumptions. But lest anyone imagine that active imagination is a way to gain "magical" power over others, let me mention that among primitives a shaman who sent out a "magic arrow" against an opponent would quickly have to construct an image of his own home or self, for if the magic arrow "missed" the enemy it would inevitably return and seek out the person who sent it. Similarly, if one sets up a psychic structure with active imagination, it may or may not modify the "enemy" but it will certainly modify the psyche of the person who does it, and perhaps not to any beneficial end.

The practice of active imagination is subtle and requires skill. It is not a technique suitable for everyone. Most often, if there is an attempt to go too far with it, the psyche will simply shift toward fantasy. It takes conscious discrimination to recognize when real active imagination is truly taking place. There is actually only one rule to help determine that—something unexpected and surprising occurs in reaction to the imaginal-ego. This is the point at which active imagination resembles the unpredictable and startling events of dreams. It shows in surprising ways the actual autonomy of the unconscious psyche.

Summary

1. Dreams in Jungian analysis are still the "royal road to the unconscious."

2. Dreams usually occur as dramatic constructions that offer the dream-ego an opportunity to deal with problems that are incompletely solved by the waking-ego.

3. Dreams are primarily in the service of individuation, and they accomplish this through compensating distorted or one-sided views held by the waking-ego.

4. The compensatory function of dreams can be seen in terms of a dialogue between the waking-ego and other aspects of the psyche, hence not all dreams are immediately related to everyday events.

5. Imaginal techniques such as sandtray constructions can be used to objectify the unconscious in much the same way as dream interpretation.

6. Internal enactments, such as hypnosis and active imagination (a unique Jungian technique) are also valuable.

7. Interpersonal enactment techniques may be used in individual analysis as well as in group psychotherapy.

Variations of Analysis

Developing slightly later than classical Freudian psychoanalysis, Jungian analysis has preserved a wide range of approaches, all more or less within the classical Jungian tradition. While the most usual setting is face to face, some Jungians, like classical Freudians, have the patient recline on a couch with the analyst sitting behind and to one side.

Some Jungians do group psychotherapy as well as one-to-one analysis, often preferring to call this "group analysis," as does Edward Whitmont, one of the pioneers of Jungian group work.[62] Others, equally respected, are opposed to group psychotherapy. The wide diversity of clinical and nonclinical backgrounds of Jungian analysts ensures continual discussion and review of the many different variations on the classic style of analysis.

Group Psychotherapy

As mentioned earlier, in chapter 1, Jung himself was not in favor of group psychotherapy. His attitude has influenced many Jungian analysts to forego that modality of treatment. Jung, however, had no experience of modern group process psychotherapy; his standpoint was based on a deep sense of the primary importance of the individual and upon the observation that in groups individuals often behave with less consciousness and responsibility than they do when acting singly.

Jung was concerned to protect the integrity of the individual in the face of pressure for group conformity. Process-oriented group psychotherapy works precisely toward that end, for it strengthens the individual's awareness of his or her own position and enables one to hold to that position in spite of pressure from a group.

My own first exposure to group psychotherapy methods came in the first year of my residency, both as a therapist of groups and as a participant in a "sensitivity-training" group. In fact, it was in the third year of my residency training that I had my first hour of

Jungian analysis—and that was while on a trip to San Francisco to a meeting of the American Group Psychotherapy Association. I have never experienced any significant contradiction between group and individual analytic work, and in fact see them as complementary. Group work is to individual analysis as laboratory work is to individual study.

Group psychotherapy is by no means a substitute for individual analysis, but a combination of group psychotherapy and individual analysis seems to move some people more rapidly in the process of growth and understanding than either modality alone. The group experience provides examples of the types of neurotic interactions that are found in one's personal history and also, often, in the symbolic statements of one's dreams. The importance of group work is in fact frequently reflected in patient's dreams, while I cannot recall an instance in which the dreams of a person in both individual analysis and group psychotherapy indicated a difficulty with the group experience.

While the individual analysis tends to constellate complexes associated with a parent figure, or a projection of the anima or animus (and more rarely the shadow), the group experience tends to produce a sense of what is acceptable or unacceptable to society as a whole. The individual analyst may have the projected role of a parent, but the group has the projected role of a family or a society.

Virtually without exception, it is easier for patients to tell a troublesome secret about themselves to the analyst rather than the group. This has advantages and disadvantages. The primary advantage, of course, is that the boundaries of the analytic container are reassuring and protective enough to permit the examination of the shadow. The negative counterpart of that, however, is that the patient often retains a sense of the unacceptability of the material even though it is accepted by the analyst. This is analogous to having a close friend who will accept the unacceptable in oneself where others—or so one thinks—still would not. Discussion of the same material in group therapy frees the patient from this different level of anxiety—the fear that he or she would be rejected by society.

With one exception, I have never seen a therapy group unanimously reject someone for material revealed in group. That lone exception was a schizoid man who threatened to put everyone in the group on his "hit list." Everyone in the group became angry and he quickly altered his bizarre fantasy.

Most often the group members are unanimous in accepting an individual's shadow, even if they don't like it and would like to see it changed. At worst, there may be a split between those accepting and rejecting, a situation that is, in itself, helpful to the patient in realizing the diversity of opinion among a group of people and in experiencing the ability to exist comfortably in the group *without* unanimous approval. One woman in a therapy group put it quite forcefully, saying that she went through life "looking for standing ovations, and if one person doesn't stand up the ovation doesn't count." Group psychotherapy helped her to some degree to take a more tolerant attitude toward herself.

From a theoretical point of view, effective group work is a powerful tool in modifying excessively rigid negative self-judgment, while simultaneously helping to develop realistic self-esteem. The same qualities of safe boundary conditions are needed for successful group psychotherapy as for individual analysis. These involve agreement between group members about the confidentiality of material that is discussed in group settings. Within those safe boundary conditions, the effective creation of affect-ego states, which reflect the unconscious psychodynamics of the group members, is a potent mode of uncovering and modifying unconscious negative self-images.

Some therapists insist on the rule that group members not socialize outside the group. Such socialization may produce alliances that interfere with the process nature of group interactions, and they may produce interactions that the persons do not want to bring back for group discussion. I have not found such a rule workable, since if adults wish to socialize to any degree outside the group, they are likely to do so despite the prohibition. What I have found important, however, is to require that any significant interaction outside the group be reported back to the group so that it can become a part of the group process. There have been rare instances in which members of a group have become sexually involved with each other, but to my knowledge these matters were subsequently always aired by the group, which acted as a firm brake on excessive acting out.

When the boundary conditions of the therapy group are respected, the process interaction between members of the group inevitably constellates powerful affect-ego states. These are most productive when they arise naturally out of the group interaction, rather than through techniques that are essentially the conduct of individual therapy in a group setting. The type of group psychotherapy that I both advocate and practice is called *process group therapy*. In process group work, the therapeutic situations are allowed to develop out of the natural interactions among persons in the group, with no use of technical "tricks" to provoke the interactions.

I have participated as an instructor or supervisor in several two-year training groups. That experience has confirmed my conviction that group psychotherapy can be an important enhancement of the experience of Jungian analysis, particularly in embodying in one's everyday life the insights obtained through individual analysis.

Marital Therapy: Archetype of the Coniunctio

Coniunctio is a term used in alchemical literature to indicate an operation in which opposites, previously existing only in a *massa confusa* (chaotic confusion), are separated and then reunited in a stable form. This is a powerful symbolic image. In some ways, all other alchemical operations are preparations for the *coniunctio*. But it is never a final end, and is followed by the preparation of a *coniunctio* of opposites at another level of the psyche, usually "higher," but sometimes "lower."

The archetypal imagery of the *coniunctio* undergirds the institution of marriage, which is a collective ceremony intended to indicate the putting together of what had been separate, in a union instituted by God, and which man is not to put asunder. Marriage rites have served social solidarity from the primitive cross-cousin marriage pattern discussed by Jung[63] to the modern world. When one has seen many couples in therapy it is possible to believe indeed that something "magical" happens with the marriage ceremony.

The magical aspect is not always as positive as it was intended to be. Time and again, partners who had a perfectly good relationship prior to marriage find that the difficulties between them began almost on the wedding night. The unconscious reason for this is fairly clear—the roles of wife and husband are vastly different from the roles of lovers. If the difficulty does not arise at the time of marriage, it may occur with the birth of the first child, for the roles of father and mother are again different from the roles of husband and wife. It is at these nodal points of difficulty that an understanding of the dual concepts of persona and anima/animus can be most crucial for the survival of the relationship.

The anima/animus, representing the principle of relationship to both the inner and the outer world, functions frequently in the service of the archetypal imagery of the *coniunctio,* indicating a state of perfect union in which the opposites function in the service of the whole without warring between themselves. The ancient Taoist symbol of the *t'ai chi tu,* already mentioned, expresses the *coniunctio* in a graphic form.

This pull toward the profound archetypal imagery of the *coniunctio,* however, while responsible for the original attraction between two persons, comes into conflict with the social roles of husband/wife and father/mother, which naturally are based on the parents, since the actual personal parents always modify and channel the archetypal potentials they unconsciously embody.

The basis of marital counseling in a Jungian framework rests largely upon two structural concepts: 1) the integration of persona roles, and 2) the relationship between anima and animus under the pressure of the unconsciously archetypal symbol of the *coniunctio.* This is a theoretical description, of course, but serves to emphasize the archetypal framework that is generally not appreciated in marital counseling.

All the analyst's skills in dealing with the anima and animus are needed when counseling a couple with difficulties. The first stage is for the partners to become aware of the point at which normal ego-functioning begins to decay into interaction between the negative anima and animus. It is only when that defensive level of communication is avoided that any real communication is possible between the two persons.

Not all Jungian analysts will see married couples or believe it is appropriate to treat both husband and wife in separate analyses at the same time. This choice depends upon both the theoretical framework of the analyst and her or his clinical training. When marriage or couple therapy is available from a Jungian analyst, however, it carries a potential depth of meaning that is profound. How profound? Profound in the sense that the appropriate focus of Jungian marital therapy is *not* the maintenance of the marriage relationship (although that may be the outcome). Instead, the primary focus is on the individuation process in each of the individuals in the marriage or relationship.

In conventional marriage or couple therapy the focus is too often on the decision of whether to stay together or to separate, whereas the real *process* that is involved is the maturation of one or both of the partners. Since this is never exactly a balanced situation—both partners are never at precisely the same growth point—it requires careful understanding of the processes in *both* to do justice to the underlying potentialities in each of them.

Jung discussed the problems of relationship in an important essay, "Marriage as a Psychological Relationship." The greater the extent of unconsciousness in one or both of the partners, he suggested, the less is marriage a matter of free conscious choice.[64] For one thing, if a person is unconscious of the actual conflicts that disturb him or her, the "cause" is frequently projected onto the partner. For another, because of the inevitable discrepancy in the psychological development of two persons, one is invariably the "container" of the process of the other.[65] In the best relationships, the roles of "container" and "contained" vary according to what is required for the development of each of the two persons.

Family Therapy

In recent years, a number of newly trained Jungian analysts have had a previous professional orientation in marriage and family therapy. There thus has been increased interest in applying Jungian principles to the treatment of families as a unit. This by no means alters the Jungian analyst's primary allegiance to the development of the individual against consuming collective pressure, whether from the family or from society. Family therapy from a Jungian perspective, therefore, focuses on the family as a matrix for the individuation of all the members. If this is not possible, the analyst may dissolve the family therapy format and work with one or more members as individuals. Because of a basic commitment to individual development, many Jungian analysts do not conduct family therapy at all.

The concept of archetypal structures, however, is in some ways quite close to the application of general systems theory to family dynamics. This approach allows one to trace unconscious patterns shared by family members. In his early work, Jung noted that members of the same family often manifested parallel response patterns in the word-association experiment, indicating that they shared similar unconscious complexes.[66] Later, Jung also pointed out that the dreams of children may sometimes compensate the family situation rather than their own developing psyches.[67]

One can readily see archetypal patterns at work in family interaction: the human sacrifice (often willing) of one family member for the "good" of the family (scapegoating), the old king and the princess as "protective" father and compliant daughter, an alliance of married sisters maintaining their unconscious childhood matriarchy against the men they married, etc. One woman dreamed of the unification of opposites in terms of feminine and masculine groupings—she dreamed she was a member of "the *brotherhood* of sisters"!

One of the saddest and most touching aspects of working with families is to see how often small children try to rescue their parents from the parents' own neurotic marriage difficulties, sacrificing themselves in the process. The altruism of the child is only partially conscious but is as striking as the observable self-centeredness of the child.

The sandtray can be as useful in picturing psychodynamics operating within the family as in showing the relationship between partners. Engaging an entire family with the sandtray construction requires some skill and guidance, but can reveal interpersonal dynamics that are difficult to bring to consciousness in verbal interactions. As Jungian analysis becomes more readily available, a Jungian approach could have a marked impact on family therapy, although the basis of Jungian work will remain the one-to-one analytic dyad.

Hypnotherapy

Early in his career, Jung himself utilized hypnosis, as did Freud, but abandoned it in favor of such techniques as dream interpretation, which he saw as "less a technique than a dialectical process between two personalities."[68] In a letter to one of his early patients, Jung writes, "I did not give up hypnosis because I wanted to avoid dealing with the basic forces of the human psyche, but because I wanted to battle with them directly and openly. . . . I gave it up simply to get rid of all the indirect advantages of this method."[69] Elsewhere Jung states that he gave up hypnosis because "I did not want to impose my will on others. . . . I wanted to protect and preserve my patient's dignity and freedom so that he could live his life by his own volition."[70]

Such remarks by Jung seem to refer primarily to the use of hypnosis as direct authoritarian suggestion for symptom removal and abreaction of emotion. Although hypnosis is still used in this manner, there are many more subtle ways of weaving it into psychoanalytic treatment, ways that preserve the values that concerned Jung and do not diminish the autonomy of the patient. Because hypnosis is primarily a collection of techniques and maxims for applying intentional suggestion in a close interpersonal framework, a therapist using hypnosis must rely upon some wider, more comprehensive theory of psychological functioning for his or her primary orientation to the clinical situation.

The field of hypnotherapy is strong on techniques, weak in theoretical understanding. The general public still often feels that hypnosis is a way for one person to control another, but properly used hypnosis is more a guided imagination process, or a meditational form, than any sort of mind-control. Some of the misconceptions are due to the misuse of hypnosis in stage presentations and in movies.

The hypnotic stunts of stage and nightclub entertainers have little to do with the serious use of hypnosis for purposes of clinical treatment. Stage "hypnosis" depends more on the self-selection of volunteers willing to perform (often even believing they actually are hypnotized). The old trick of showing that a person is hypnotized by making him rigid and placing him across two chairs, the shoulders on one chair and ankles on the other, actually simply demonstrates a little-known ability of virtually anyone. Holding that position uses the largest and strongest muscles of the body—the same muscles that are used in maintaining upright posture against the pull of gravity.

In a major review of the theories of hypnosis, Harold Crasilneck and myself have directed attention to what we call the *psycho-structural* aspects of hypnosis theory.[71] By this we mean to emphasize that whatever theories of hypnosis are used, they must be consistent with the structure of the mind and the brain. Hypnosis is a way of utilizing the unrecognized abilities of the human mind, but it relies upon other theories of the mind and is not itself an independent view.

Hypnotherapists, therefore, use a collection of hypnotic techniques, but must apply them within whatever theoretical structure of the mind they affirm. That larger theoretical structure does not come directly from the field of hypnosis, but from other views that are applied to the clinical application of hypnosis. For that reason, there should be no independent field of hypnotherapists who have no fundamental clinical training other than their training in hypnosis. An independent field of hypnosis would be like training students to pull teeth without having to go to dental school to learn what to do if there are complications.

The Jungian view of the mind is especially useful in understanding and applying hypnotherapy techniques. As the most comprehensive theoretical model of the mind yet available, the Jungian view allows the therapist to better understand the dynamic meaning of the hypnotic interaction, particularly in imagery produced in the hypnotic state.

The hypnotic state is produced more by the patient than by the hypnotherapist, who can only give suggestions that are likely to facilitate entering a trance state. In Jungian terms, the boundary conditions of the patient's waking-ego are more immediately and directly controlled by the hypnotic suggestions, allowing the patient's ego to enter a state similar to active imagination (but more properly called a *guided imagination* because the suggestions of the therapist come from outside the patient's own mind).

Even in a light hypnotic state, it is possible for a good subject to experience an autonomy of imagery that is difficult in waking life. In the waking state, what is represented by the images is more likely to appear as subtle changes in the emotional background tone of consciousness; to perceive these requires much more attention and awareness than most untrained people have. As in dreams, the images that appear in valid hypnotherapy represent the movement and interaction of complexes in the unconscious mind—the same complexes that affect the structure and quality of self-image when the patient is in ordinary consciousness.

The same skills that are developed in dream analysis can be directly applied to understanding this imagery. In a technique called the *affect-bridge,* introduced into hypnotherapy by John Watkins,[72] the similarity of affective tone is used to identify memories from different stages of life that are related to the same meaning—or in Jungian terms, that have the same underlying complex pattern. Contact with complexes in the guided imagination of the hypnotic state naturally produces affective responses, just as does contact with complexes in waking life or in the word-association experiment.

These affect-ego states can be more finely controlled in hypnosis than in waking interaction. The analysand in hypnosis can be asked to identify with the imagery arising in the mind, but can also be told to *dis*identify from the imagery if the resulting affect is too disturbing. This is not a suggestion to totally and forever avoid contact with that imagery, but to withdraw from it at that moment. Repeated contact with the imagery is used, much like desensitization in behavioral therapy, until the ego is able to assimilate the contents of the complex without being overwhelmed.

For example, a person might have had a disturbing dream, one in which the dream-ego felt alone and abandoned. After inducing an appropriate level of hypnotic trance, the subject would be asked to revivify the dream until it acquired a degree of verisimilitude, a likeness to the original dream experience. Then a suggestion might be given to "keep the feelings, but let the scene fade away." Then the subject in hypnosis would be asked to "go back in time, backward in time, a part of your mind going back in time, until you find another memory, another scene, that has the *same feeling tone,* the same feelings." Usually the subject will have been instructed to indicate that such a memory has been identified by raising one designated finger.

The suggestion is then given to recreate and experience the second memory, and so on, continuing as long as such exploration seems productive. The memories are then examined, in the hypnotic or waking state or in both. One can often observe similarities in the remembered events. Usually they cluster about some common denominator, perhaps a trauma to the patient's self-esteem. The original dream, for example, might involve anxiety about not being prepared for an examination in college. Using the affect of anxiety as a bridge, the second memory might be of discovering at a party in high school that one's girlfriend was flirting with another man. A third memory might be ridicule by one's father for a childhood transgression. The identification of various memories having the same emotional tone provides an excellent area for analytical investigation.

Hypnosis can be used in many ways other than the exploration of imagery. Hypnosis is a powerful tool in interrupting unhealthy habit patterns, such as smoking or compulsive overeating, and in the lessening of intractable pain, as in some cases of terminal disease. These uses of hypnosis derive little from Jungian understanding, although the Jungian model is helpful in managing the accompanying transference-countertransference aspects.

There are disadvantages as well as advantages to the use of hypnotherapy. Some people are not good hypnotic subjects. Although repeated trials of hypnotic induction may enable such a person to enter more deeply into a trance state, it may be insufficient for practical results. Hypnotherapy does not necessarily move more rapidly than other forms of psychotherapy. The induction and maintenance of the hypnotic state require a significant amount of the therapist's time. Furthermore, the material produced in hypnotic trance, while valuable, is not from as deep a level of the mind as are dreams. Understanding derived from the imagery of hypnotherapy must still be applied by the waking personality, which may require individual or group psychotherapy as well.

Hypnosis can also accelerate the development of transference reactions, which if marked must be dealt with in a conventional psychotherapeutic manner. I have in mind a case in which the sudden eruption of a negative transference (in a patient who usually had a positive relationship to the therapist) occurred when a dream was being explored under light hypnosis. In that instance it was possible to see dramatically the manner in which the analysand unknowingly identified himself with a figure in the dream, while simultaneously identifying the therapist with a persecutory figure in the same dream. It took more than forty-eight hours to sort out this distortion of the patient's normal consciousness, caused by identification with the complexes in the dream. At that point, the material uncovered by this experience proved useful in the ongoing analytic process. Such events, however, are obviously undesirable if they occur in situations where the therapist is untrained in dealing with unconscious material and its impact upon the transformative field.

Freud abandoned hypnosis because the abreactive improvement obtained through discharge of emotional memories during hypnosis did not persist. Jung abandoned hypnosis because he did not understand how it effected a cure.[73] Both Freud and Jung, therefore, desired a deeper understanding of the unconscious processes involved in the phenomena of hypnosis. It remains a valuable and impressive tool in the armamentarium of the clinician. The future integration of hypnotic techniques and Jungian theory will facilitate even further the applications of hypnotherapy within the context of classical Jungian analysis and dream interpretation.

Although I now utilize hypnotherapy in only a small percentage of cases, I do not find its careful use incompatible with dream interpretation and other more traditional Jungian techniques. I dare to imagine that Jung himself might agree, were he alive and aware of the developments in the understanding of hypnosis since his early days with Freud.

Summary

1. As Jungian analysis becomes a more established field of practice, it will find wider application in treatment modalities other than the classical one-to-one approach. These developments will be informed and guided by the understanding of the psyche provided by classical analysis.

2. Jungian analysts trained in other techniques can both enrich the field of analytical psychology and bring the deeper understanding of the psyche, derived from Jungian experience, to a wider range of clinical application.

"In the interaction between them, mother and infant together form the emotional bonding essential to a meaningful relationship." (Photo courtesy Jessie, left, and Vicki)

8

The Individuating Ego

Analysis is a formal process of self-reflection and understanding, meant to free one from unnecessary bondage to complexes that are dominant in one's personal psychology. Jungian analysis is also intended to help one find the path of one's own individuation, which can never be defined in general or cultural terms. Analysis is a window upon individuation. Individuation is deeper life. Meaningful life is the goal.

The Personal and the Transpersonal

As infants we enter a world that is vastly complex, and yet there are patterns of behavior between infant and mother that bring the newborn into profound relationship with the mother. Observations of early mother-child interaction have shown the surprisingly early transactions that are meant to forge emotional bonds. The newborn will turn its face toward the cheek that is touched by a hand—the so-called rooting reflex—probably an innate response to help the infant find the nourishing breast. This response from the infant also has an emotional impact on the nursing mother. In the interaction between them, mother and infant together form the emotional bonding essential to a meaningful relationship.

Observation of infants in the first year of life has shown that an infant will at first respond with a smile to a pattern of the human face, at times even to a cardboard cutout that shows only eyes, forehead, eyebrows and nose. This is analogous to the experimental observation that newly hatched chicks will crouch when a cardboard form of a hawk is pulled forward on a wire above them, but will not respond if the same form is pulled over them tail-first. These are innate patterns which relate the newborn to the surrounding environment.

At about the midpoint of the first year of life, however, the child will begin to respond differentially, smiling when the mother's face is seen but showing displeasure with the presentation of a strange face. This may well be the beginning of the emergence of a personal sphere of interaction out of the original undifferentiated unity of the child's world. Although we are born with innate potentials (and no two of us are exactly equal in that regard), we live them out in the context of a personal world that is constructed from family, social and cultural interactions. The beginning of this personal drama, the life story that each of us weaves, begins when the infant responds differentially to the mother.

We emerge from an archetypal world and construct a personal world for ourselves out of whatever materials we are given by fate and circumstance. The mother carries for the infant all the archetypal possibilities of the archetype of the mother, presumably formed over immense time by the unconscious assimilation in the species of the inexpressible mass experience of human mothering. These archetypal possibilities are gradually incorporated, to whatever degree possible, into the developing image of the personal mother. But no actual mother can be an adequate carrier for the extended range of possibilities of the archetypal mother. Both infant and mother are unaware of this process, feeling the relationship is only between them. In later life, however, in dreams and imaginal productions, it is possible to observe that the archetypal possibilities not realized by the personal mother are still present in the psyche, ready to enrich the mind in ways that were not sufficiently realized in childhood.

Dream images that show mothering figures other than the personal mother often indicate the attempt of these archetypal patterns to contact the ego. The same is true, of course, of the archetype of the father. These internal pressures for the experience of parental imagos behind the image of the personal parents account for a large part of positive transference upon the analyst.

A woman whose relationship with her personal mother was unsatisfactory, even in childhood, had a number of experiences after the suicide of her husband that showed an attempt by her psyche to awaken the positive aspect of the archetype of the mother—the aspect that had been insufficiently experienced with her personal mother. In one waking experience, she had a vision of the Virgin Mary during mass. In a dream, she experienced Mary crying; in the same dream she experienced a brief reunion with her dead husband.

By adulthood, it is usual for the human being to have no memory of the earliest years of life, a time when the everyday world of

familiar surroundings was constructed out of archetypal potentialities. Those possibilities which were actualized are felt to be
"real," and those that remain dormant in the unconscious have no
existence at all in the conscious mind, although they may be powerful patterns that will be needed later in life.

In its usual state, the adult human mind is aware of the immen-
sities of the physical universe and the vast numbers of other persons
in the world, but relatively unaware of the range and complexity of
the objective psyche within. It is usually only the introverted personality, or the extravert who through force of individuation develops introversion in the second half of life, that is aware of the
reality of the inner world. The personal sphere of the individual is
transcended both inwardly and outwardly by transpersonal realities.
To the puer who tends to identify with unactualized potentialities,
the objective demands of the external world are an antidote to
dangerous flights of inflation that would hold the person back from
actualization of life. For the person too overwhelmed by the ten
thousand things of the external world, the perception of the inner
universe is a refreshing and welcome contrast.

Mankind is obliged to live in both worlds, holding the tension
that inevitably arises between them. In looking at a large number
of analytical cases over decades, it has seemed clear to me that the
Self desires two achievements: 1) the formation of a strong ego,
and 2) that the ego, once formed, again relate to the depths of the
psyche. If the person holds back from life (a usual cause of
neurosis), the dreams seem to press for a working through of that
resistance. In a serious blockage, the dreams may even become
threatening to the dream-ego, as if to push where persuasion has
failed. While neurosis may appear to be only an impediment to
living a complete life, it actually has a positive purpose in that its
symptoms force the ego to face up to the avoided tasks of individuation.

Once there is a strong ego structure, dreams often reveal possibilities of relating more deeply to the unconscious. Dreams of
initiation may occur at that time. It is as if the regulating center of
the psyche, the Self, presses for the development of an ego structure
in order to establish a viewpoint in the world. The Self *then* presses
for the depths of the psyche to be seen. In short, the psyche wishes
to see itself!

Only a strongly developed personality can withstand the tensions of seeing deeply into the unconscious. Jung was such a personality, a powerful model, according to Edward Edinger, of how man is to exist in the age to come—standing firmly on earth, while contemplating both the starry heavens that surround us outside and the vastness of the objective psyche within.[74] Mankind is the only form of life yet known that can bear the tension of these two universes, and perhaps bring them into harmonious relationship. Through the work of mankind, the universe may become more conscious of itself. And the *only* known carrier of this immense process is the individual human being toiling in the personal and unique process of individuation.

Circumambulation of the Self

Based partly on parallels to yoga, but primarily upon his own experiences and dreams, Jung conceived of the process of individuation as a circumambulation ("walking around") of the archetypal Self by the ego.[75] Like a point on the periphery of a wheel, the ego feels that it is continually circling the "still point," the hub of the wheel, the Self. It is as if all of our experience were a part of the life of the Self. We are incapable of immediately experiencing the totality of meaning of our own individual lives, although we can be intuitively aware that we move about (circumambulate) a virtual center of meaning, the archetypal Self.

Circumambulation is an age-old ritual for showing respect to sacred shrines and objects. In traditional Tibet, the Buddhist temples were circumambulated in a clockwise direction (symbolic of increasing consciousness) and the shamanistic Bon temples were circumambulated in the reverse, counterclockwise direction.

It seems to me that an image of the centered Self is caught in T.S. Eliot's phrase "at the still point of the turning world," from "Burnt Norton," the first of his *Four Quartets*. The imagery continues, seeming to express the ambiguity of the archetypal Self, in these lines:

    . . . Neither flesh nor fleshless;
Neither from nor towards; . . .
But neither arrest nor movement. And do not call it fixity,
    . . . Neither ascent nor decline. . . .

Eliot adds: "Except for the point, the still point,/There would be no dance, and there is only the dance."[76]

As the maker of dreams, the archetypal Self continually confronts the ego with symbolic dream images of itself. The ego sees its egocentric illusions mirrored in the larger vision of the Self, a mirroring that is most often gentle, even amused. A man told of participating in a panel discussion of several unusual films at a meeting of a humanistic psychology organization. Although he was tired, and had to push himself to muster energy for the evening, he felt himself to be an excellent panelist—witty, succinct, pithy—and was well applauded and frequently congratulated at the end of the evening. But what did the Self as dream-maker think of his wonderful performance? That very night he dreamed that he had been masturbating in public!

At a crucial time in my own life I had a dream that seemed like a mere gluttonous wish-fulfillment—a large cone of ice cream on which were sprinkled chopped-up dates from a palm tree. And what was this concoction called in the dream?—a Palm Sundae! My association to Palm *Sunday* was "a momentary triumph preceding a painful crucifixion." I was too young and inexperienced at the time to correctly understand or heed the gentle, almost amused warning in my dream. But sure enough, I was subsequently "crucified" by an enormous conflict. Fortunately, this involved not just the motif of crucifixion, but the larger theme of death-and-transformation. The painful events that the Palm Sundae dream foreshadowed led to necessary and profound changes that were long overdue.

The tone of these two dreams, where fun is poked at the ego in a quite serious way, gives a flavor of how the Self deals with the ego when one is seriously trying to find a way amid the many options of individuation. Looking at many such dreams from a large number of analysands, I have an impression of the Self as wiser and older, a benevolent friend. The Self seems always concerned with the state of the ego, yet almost infinitely patient and nonjudgmental of the ego's false turnings.

"Negative" Forms of the Unconscious

The unconscious can show a harsh and apparently negative face when the ego continually avoids a necessary step in development. In such situations, there frequently occur dreams in which something or someone is trying to break into a house where the ego lives. At times, the intruder is shown as primitive—an elephant, an ape, an unnaturally large spider, etc. I have also seen dream images of a primitive mounted warrior, Indians on the warpath, large malevolent machines, vampires and so on. It is characteristic of this type of dream that the intruding figure usually does not actually try to harm the ego, but insists upon entry. Similar intrusions occur in the imagery of authentic active imagination when the ego is in need of movement.

At an art exhibit, a man was fascinated with a strange painting of a sailing ship with a large spider covering the billowing sail. Later, in active imagination, he tried to reproduce the painting in his mind as a dramatic scene, with himself in a small boat alongside, in order to understand the fascination of the image. To his horror, the spider came down from the mast and pursued him across the water, apparently to devour him. At the last moment, however, it turned over, revealing its female genitalia. With surprise, he realized that its true intent was to be fertilized so that it might reproduce. Among many other archetypal meanings—the most common of which is the negative and devouring mother—the spider also means the spinner of the world, who spins the world out of itself— the image of Maya, creator of illusion.

Another man reported running through Central Park in New York, under the influence of drugs, with the delusion that a large black spider was on his head. Sympathetically I exclaimed how frightening that must have been for him. No, he explained, the spider was trying to pick a hole in the top of his head that somehow would help him. This man was unaware of the Tibetan tantric yoga practice designed to produce an "opening" in the top of the head to permit the soul to escape the body at the moment of death.

It is not only in dream imagery that the Self may deal harshly with the ego. It sometimes seems that if the ego insists on avoiding a necessary step in the process of individuation, the Self can initiate an involuntary form of the needed experience. A quite extraverted man, who in midlife continually refused to pause and examine the meaning of his life, badly fractured his leg while skiing and was forced to be inactive for several months. During this forced inactivity, he finally began to consider the neglected introverted side of himself. One can never be certain, of course, that such accidents are unconsciously determined rather than simply the result of "cause and effect," but the accumulation of many observations leads me to be cautious in dismissing lightly such apparently meaningful coincidences.

The etiology of psychosomatic illnesses is less in dispute. It is apparent in many cases that neglecting to deal with a serious unconscious conflict can lead finally to physical illness.[77] Except when expressed in the voluntary musculature system, as in the hysterical paralysis of an extremity, inability to talk, etc., the illness does not seem to be a direct symbolic expression of the underlying conflict. Rather, the illness is mediated through the body's chronic reaction to the emotions generated by the suppressed conflict. But overstatement of this psychosomatic hypothesis can lead to unnecessary and useless guilt. I have seen a man dying of cancer confronted by his "therapist" with the probing question, "Why do you *want* to die?" Even if there is a psychological component to cancer, by the time physical alteration of the body has occurred, the condition cannot responsibly be dealt with by psychology alone.

Both the positive and negative forms in which the Self appears to the ego seem to be in the service of individuation. In the very long perspective of, say, a lengthy analysis, virtually everything can be seen as serving the mysterious process of circumambulation of the Self, a circular and sometimes serpentine way with turnings back and confusing loops, but nevertheless a directed and moving process—*if* seen in suitable perspective. Barbara Hannah, a Zurich analyst who trained directly with Jung, once remarked in her old age that the basic value of a long life was to see the outcome of so many other lives! With such a perspective, the positive and negative images of the Self seem to coalesce and meld into a pattern that cannot be precisely defined within conventional categories of conscious thought, and yet is deeply meaningful and coherent.

The ego apparently has no choice as to whether it will acknowledge and interact with the archetypal Self, but it does have a choice in terms of the quality of the interaction. The Self can be circumambulated in a reverent, concerned but independent manner—or the ego can be forced through illness, disruptions of ordinary consciousness and symbolic images (including both dreams and "accidents") to give attention to the unlived aspects of individuation that are the concern of the Self.

And what is the purpose of this circumambulation of the Self? Once more, Eliot furnishes a poetic image for what is difficult of description in prose. In "Little Gidding," the conclusion of the *Four Quartets,* he suggests that after a completed journey one knows one's origins for the first time, perhaps as part of a circumambulated totality:

> We shall not cease from exploration
> And the end of all our exploring
> Will be to arrive where we started
> And know the place for the first time.[78]

Later, in the same concluding verse, this wholeness is called "a condition of complete simplicity/(Costing not less than every-thing)."[79]

Mandala Forms

One of the symbolic forms in which the archetypal Self appears is as a mandala. Mandalas are a traditional meditational form in both Buddhist and Hindu yoga. Traditional images are arranged in a centered pattern, often combining a square and a circle, and usually divided into four quadrants. In each quadrant, a religious figure was placed, while in the center of the mandala was the principle figure of which they were aspects. A Christian form of the mandala would have Christ in the center, with the four apostles, perhaps in their symbolic animal forms, in the four quadrants. A similar motif in ancient Egyptian theology might consist of Horus surrounded by his four sons.

Jung used the term mandala to describe images he found in the dreams and unconscious creations of his patients. In this psychological usage, mandala refers to an image that shows a centered pattern in which both the periphery and the center are emphasized. Using this definition, mandalas can often be seen in dreams: a cubical building with a fountain in the center, an empty town square with a building at each corner, a square cookie with a large candied fruit in its center, etc.

The mandala represents an extremely ordered presentation of the archetypal Self. It is therefore more likely to occur spontaneously when the ego is in need of centering. I have at times seen most remarkable examples of this spontaneous production of mandala symbolism in the sandtray. Years ago I was shown the finger-paint-ings of a woman who entered a hospital in a dissociated schizophrenic state. She reconstituted a stable personality while in the hospital and was discharged. When she was the most unstable, just after admission, her finger-paintings were of almost pure mandala forms. As her ego became more stable, the finger-paintings took on a more fluid character.

In this instance, as in others, it is as if the unconscious wishes there to be an ego strong enough to withstand unconscious pressure, and attempts to compensate for a weak ego with increased images of order in the unconscious. This compensatory effort can fail, of course, in which case the ego would be overwhelmed by unconscious contents, as in acute schizophrenia.

Crucifixion and Enlightenment: The Cross and the Bodhi Tree

Long before the rise of psychoanalysis at the beginning of the twentieth century, the great religious systems offered their answers to the perennial human questions of mankind's place in the universe and how to live a meaningful life. Many systems of religious thought have come and gone, and many remain.

Of the world's living religions, Islam, Judaism and Christianity are "children of the book," having some traditions and scriptural figures in common, even with their varying interpretations. Buddhism is in some ways more a psychology than a religion, having no specific conception of deity. Yet it functions to give meaning and understanding of the mystery of existence for millions of people. There are divisions and subdivisions within all the great religions, and at times animosity is greater among variants of a faith than between different religious faiths themselves. Pink is the enemy of red, as they say, not of blue.

Years ago I had a spontaneous vision that seemed to me to involve both Christian and Buddhist imagery. It occurred at a time of great personal tension, and also at a time when I wondered if I would physically survive. My mind involuntarily posed the question: When Christ on the cross said, "My God, My God, Why hast Thou forsaken me?"—what did God reply? As quickly as the question posed itself, the spontaneous answer came (with a sense of shock at the change in tone). In my vision, God said, "Just relax for a minute, Honey, and you'll drop right off!"

The vision faded as quickly as it had come. But it was disquieting, to say the least (like my earlier vision, discussed in the introduction, of Jung as a rocket ship propelled by excrement). Was the vision sacrilegious? I was almost afraid to examine it for fear of what I would find. But then, when I did open myself to the implications, it immediately seemed clear that the central image of Christianity was the crucifixion of Christ, and the most significant moment of that event was Christ's reported cry at being abandoned by God. The "reply" from God seemed out of place. And yet—. It suddenly came to me that in my spontaneous vision Christ's question had been voiced in the tradition of Christianity, while God's answer had been from a Buddhist perspective.

In the Buddhist view, all suffering of old age, illness and death is somehow the result of desire. No desire, no loss. Even the fear of death might vanish if one had no desire to cling to life. The implication of the vision was the thought, new to me then, that Christ was more a willing participant than I had imagined, that he had to strain to "hold" to the cross, and that if he had relaxed (in Buddhist terms, "let go") he would have "dropped off."

The idea of Christ voluntarily holding on to the cross, rather than being forcibly nailed to it, is strikingly pictured in Salvador Dali's painting *Christ of St. John of the Cross*, which has always astounded me with its spiritual implications. The perspective is most unusual: the crucifixion scene floats in the air like a spiritual image, while it is viewed as if by someone in heaven looking down on the head of Christ.

At a recent meeting of the International Society of Hypnosis in the art museum in Glasgow, Scotland, there were only a few minutes before closing to visit the exhibits. I was surprised to "accidentally" find Dali's original painting hanging at the end of a long balcony corridor. As seems to be always true, the original painting conveyed so much more than the reproductions and prints I had seen. The psychological implication that flooded into my mind was that Christ's crucifixion, the central image of Christianity, was a profound image of transformation through suffering, an image not just of death but of death-transformation-rebirth.

In contrast, the central image of Buddhism is Gautama Buddha in meditation, sometimes under the bodhi tree where he achieved enlightenment after giving up useless ascetic practices that had almost killed him. This central Buddhist image is of transformation through "letting go." Thus, the central image of Christianity is of transformation through extreme fixation and suffering, while that of Buddhism is of transformation through extreme letting go.

Christ of St. John of the Cross, by Salvador Dali, 1951.
(Art Gallery, Glasgow)

And yet, these two great religious images are really opposite sides of one underlying process. They seem like two different alchemical operations, *mortificatio* and *solutio*, psychologically similar to mortification and dissociation. Both operations are necessary in the formation of the Philosophers' Stone, an image of the highest, most enduring value, capable of transmuting lesser values into itself, "turning lead into gold." In psychological terms, transformation through fixation and suffering and transformation through letting go are both necessary at various times in life. Together they make a more complete model for transforming the ordinary human condition than does either alone.

I am still unsure of all the implications of this vision, now years in the past. But the effect and immediacy of its impact on me has not lessened. I take great hope in the beginning of serious Buddhist-Christian dialogue—not in the technical and theological arguments, rather in the juxtaposition of their imagery, the moving quality of their great religious images. The Risen Christ and the Compassionate Buddha may prove to be complementary images of the Way.

Preparation for Death

As the goal of the first half of life is the establishment of a strong ego in the world, so the goal of the second half of life is reconciling the ego to the meaning of life in the face of inevitable death.

To ignore the task of ego-growth in the first half of life is as out of step with the natural movement of life as is ignoring the inevitability of death as the "goal" of the second half of life. Jung stated that the correct way to end life was to carry on as if one had a thousand years of life, to literally "live oneself right out of life."[80] But that seems an impossible prescription for the ego that sees death as the total annihilation of all that is known, all that matters in the world.

Experience with many dreams gives the impression that dreams are made by a part of us, theoretically the archetypal Self, that is in some ways far larger than the ego-personality with which we usually identify. The dream-making part of us again and again proves wiser and more understanding than the ego-personality, and it is certainly not less than the ego. The unconscious is clearly more than the mere repository of repressed wishes and drives ("the demands the body makes upon the mind") that Freud postulated in his nineteenth-century mechanistic model of the psyche.

And how does the dream-making part of us, the Self, view the overwhelming question of death? If dreams are the self-representation of the psyche, and if they function in a compensatory way to balance consciousness, how do dreams themselves view death?

Dreams *prepare* the psyche for death. But dreams seem to view death in no more dramatic terms than a journey, a marriage or some other major change in life. Freud could have explained this away by theorizing that the unconscious, having had no experience of death, does not represent it in dreams. But it is more mysterious than Freud's reductionistic viewpoint. It is as if the dreams of someone approaching physical death were no more concerned about the approaching death than they would be about any major change *within life*.

Several years ago, a close friend died of cancer. She knew she was in a terminal state and had chosen to have no more medical treatment, returning to her home. During the last weeks, I visited with her almost daily. The chief topic of our conversation was her dreams. She had never been a patient of mine and to my knowledge had never had formal psychotherapy, but she was deeply interested in the nature of life and in dreams. At the time of her death, she had two teenage sons, one of whom worried her. She was particularly concerned as to what might happen to that son after her death.

In a dream about two weeks before she died, she found herself, together with the son she was concerned about, at a very fancy clinic for the treatment of mothers and problem sons. The treatment consisted of lying down with the son on a large metal ottoman that was covered with intricate "Hindu" engravings. The ottoman then rotated and rose gently into the air. If it dipped downward suddenly, which did not hurt either the mother or the son, it was a sign that the son would eventually be fine. In the dream, she and her son lay on the ottoman, it rotated and rose into the air, and it dropped suddenly. From that moment on, she gave up her worry about the son's future after her own death. The dream gently allowed her to relinquish a sense of responsibility for her son, preparing her in that manner for her own death.

The final dream that we discussed prior to her death was of a horse race. Horses were getting into position for the beginning of a race which had not yet started. Her dream-ego was excited and interested. This would seem to be a dream preparing the psyche for death. If one realizes that the body may be represented in dreams by an animal, frequently a horse,[81] the dream said that her body was getting ready to run a race, actually its final race. She herself was not in the race, but was watching with interest. This dream occurred within about twelve hours of her physical death.

Later I learned that before she died my friend had broken into profuse sweating. She had asked her nurse, a kindly old black woman who had known her many years, "Mary, am I having death-sweats?" The nurse had soothingly reassured her that she was not, although the nurse had attended other dying persons and knew that this profuse sweating might precede death. The sweating was like the last race of her body, using all the mechanisms of the autonomic nervous system in a final and impossible attempt to prolong life. I had not until then heard of "death-sweats," but on inquiry found that it was part of the wisdom of folk language in rural Texas.

Soon after this woman died, a mutual friend came to me with a dream she did not understand. In the dream, the dead friend had come to her door with an unknown man and had given her some pennies with the instruction that they were to be given to James Hall. The dreamer had no associations to the pennies. But *I* did! Several years before her death, my friend, her husband, myself and another friend had been in England on the last day that the old-style large English pennies were in circulation as currency. My friend's husband had bought some old penny-arcade machines that worked only with these large English pennies. He was going from bank to bank, collecting sacks of them (very heavy!) to bring back to the United States for his arcade machines. We had spent an afternoon carrying these heavy sacks of English pennies around with us.

It was as if the dream were sent to reassure me about her continued existence after bodily death. It was even more impressive that the dream came through a third party who did not know the meaning of the pennies, the central motif of the dream. A sceptic, of course, could hypothesize that the dreamer unconsciously learned of the pennies through telepathy or clairvoyance and also unconsciously formulated the dream for my benefit. I prefer to believe that my friend was sending a message about her survival of death, and sending it through a third party in such a way that I would not consider it simply a subjective part of my own memory of her.

Beyond Death

We do not know if there is anything beyond death. Perhaps the body simply returns to its component elements and the personality ceases to exist. But the immemorial belief of mankind is that something of human personality does survive physical death.

Records of some of the earliest human burials show that the dead person was placed in a foetal position in the grave, as if awaiting rebirth. In recent years, scientific investigation of early cave burial sites has shown that the pollen count is greater in the dirt of early gravesites than in the surrounding area. This suggests that even in prehistoric times the human being was often buried with flowers, perhaps an indication of ceremonial burial and hope that death was not the final end.

In 1882 the Society for Psychical Research was formed at Cambridge University in England. Its purpose was to investigate with the methods of science the abilities of the human being that had been asserted by religious traditions—abilities such as telepathy, clairvoyance and the possibility of surviving physical death. One of the early publications by F.W.H. Myers, a founder of the SPR, was called *Human Personality and Its Survival of Bodily Death.*[82] The SPR continues, together with its younger American counterpart, the ASPR, to investigate such questions. Although research in parapsychology has progressed greatly, the question of human survival of death has become more complicated. Evidence that the living human being is capable of telepathy and clairvoyance makes it more difficult to scientifically assess messages that seem to come from deceased persons—in the present terminology, from "incorporeal personal agencies."

It is one of the ironies of modern life that mankind's oldest question, the meaning of death and possible life beyond the grave, receives so little scientific investigation when the implications for such study are so immense. Knowing with some certainty that there is survival of some part of the human personality beyond death might revolutionize civilization.

Dream Evidence

Before his mother died, Jung had a dream that he did not understand at the time.[83] In the dream his father, long dead, came to ask him about the latest methods of marriage therapy, which Jung told him. It was only when his mother died soon after that Jung realized the dream might have been a representation of his father's surviving personality trying to prepare itself for reunion with Jung's mother.

Jung was on a trip when he received news of his mother's death. That night he dreamed of a large terrifying wolf tearing through the forest in search of a human soul—a sense of the terror and brutality of death.[84] Returning the next day to Zurich for his mother's funeral, Jung noted that in the background of his mind he kept hearing wedding music. To him this music represented another meaning of death—as if it were a reunion and putting together, a happy time like a wedding. Thus Jung recorded his experiences of the two contrasting meanings of death.

Just before my own father died in 1975, he told my sister the only dream that anyone in the family remembers him ever reporting to any of us. He told her he had dreamed he was going to visit a certain aunt and uncle, the couple that he had gone to live with for a year when he completed high school. It had been the turning point of his early years, when he was able to gather himself together and prepare for life. We did not know at the time that he was ill, nor did he, but the dream seemed to be preparing him for death with an image he would understand—the image of a safe place to go when you have to leave home. In his associations, it would also have symbolized a place one *chooses* to go in order to start a new phase of life.

Soon after my father died, my sister and I both dreamed of him. I dreamed I was sitting in the breakfast room of the house where I had grown up, working on papers having to do with my father's estate, when he walked into the room carrying his suitcase, which I recognized, as if he were returning from a trip. He greeted me warmly, then went to find my mother and sister to say hello to them. My sister dreamed that he was sitting at a large round table with some other people she did not know, enjoying himself. She hugged him and passed on through the room.

Such dreams, not at all uncommon, are of course not proof of life after death; indeed, one might argue that they are "sent" by the Self simply to give some comfort to those still living. Death is the final step of individuation as known by living human personalities, but perhaps that psychic structure we call the Self has a more inclusive and far-reaching perspective.

9

Beyond Analysis: Scientific and Religious
Implications of Jungian Theory

Jung and Freud

Jung and Freud were more than psychiatrists concerned with treating the disturbed mind. They were ultimately concerned with the nature of reality and man's place in the universe. Both tacitly believed that understanding the depths of the mind would at the same time reveal truths about the nature of reality itself. Yet the intuitive answers they offered about the nature of the unconscious were vastly different.

Freud came at last to a dual instinct theory—the life instinct opposing the death instinct, libido against thanatos. Freud's theory is finally pessimistic: the forces of life and pleasure can only hold at bay for a brief time the inexorable triumph of the death instinct. All organic life returns to inorganic elements. For Freud, life is finally a tragedy, a brief epiphenomenal dance above the abyss of death. The materialistic tone of Freud's theory reflects nineteenth-century European scientism, not science as it exists today. This was Freud's faith and he lived and died in it with heroic bravery, ever defending the truth as he saw it, while suffering with fortitude his last painful illness and decline.

At the deepest layer of the mind, Freud had seen only the instincts pressing for discharge, the pressures that the body places upon the mind. Freud called this aspect of the mind the *id*, the "it." The ego or conscious mind and the superego or conscience—the other parts of the mind in Freudian theory—carry a sense of structure and content.[85] The id carries more a sense of pressure, like a hydraulic pump simply driving the more conscious parts of the mind to achieve discharge, without understanding or knowledge of the complexities and requirements of the conscious social world.

For a brief time when I was a psychiatry resident, I became quite concerned about the id, since it did not seem to have the same structural elements as the ego and the superego, with which it was parallel as a structural concept. For several days I asked all my

137

professors about the structure of the id, ending with no more knowledge than I began.

The id does have a theoretical structure, of course, and is roughly analogous to the Jungian structural concept of the shadow. But in Jungian theory there are many layers of the mind beyond the shadow. In particular, it is the concept of the collective unconscious, which Jung later renamed the objective psyche, that basically distinguishes Jungian theory from the Freudian model of the psyche.

The Jungian Psyche

Jung's model of the psyche assigns a creative, essentially positive meaning to the deepest layer of the unconscious mind. This is the objective psyche, as real in its own way as the external physical world. In fact, its archetypal predispositions structure not only the inner subjective world, but to a great degree our perception of the external world as well. Whereas the "contents" of the personal unconscious are complexes (both normal and at times pathological), the "contents" of the objective psyche are the archetypes, coordinated by the central archetype of order, the Self. *The objective psyche is the matrix of human consciousness.* Ordering is intrinsic to it, but it is a dynamic and unfolding order, not a static and unchanging structure. In this dynamic order lies the genesis of the individuation process, the basic activity of incarnating in a human life the potentialities of the unique Self of the individual.

Although Jung's is a basically positive view, he is by no means merely optimistic. Human life is real, embodying real successes and equally real failures. Even the life of mankind on the planet Earth can succeed or fail. But there is no intrinsic tragedy in Jung's model of the structure of the psyche. There is no inevitable triumph of a "death instinct." Although death is undeniable, the deeper layers of the psyche, as indicated in the previous chapter, act as if death is not a crucial event. It may be that as life shows increasing entropic disorder on the physical plane, it also exhibits increasing complexity of pattern on the level of meaning and understanding. We are in the dark ages as far as understanding ourselves or the universe we inhabit. Yet lack of knowledge is not the same as despair. There are scientific and religious implications of the Jungian experience that give reason for hope.

Religious Implications

Freud titled his work on religion *The Future of an Illusion*. This indicates his basic attitude toward religion, although some writers, among them David Bakan, have suggested that Freud unconsciously was more influenced than he realized by his own religious tradition.[86]

Jung's view of religion was again in direct contrast to Freud's theoretical pessimism regarding the opposition of eros and thanatos. Jung said that he had never treated a person in the second half of life who did not have a religious problem. By "religious problem" Jung did not mean difficulty with doctrinal questions or with the institutional church, but rather a problem of meaning, of understanding a purpose to life, a reason for living.

Jung's own father was a pastor in the Swiss Reformed Church, and Jung describes in a moving way the essentially stagnant end of his father's religious life.[87] When Jung as a boy was listening eagerly to his father's explanation of religious concepts, he was deeply and tragically disappointed when they came to the mysterious concept of the Trinity, which Jung had been eagerly anticipating. His father skipped over it, explaining that he did not really understand it himself. In a real sense, Jung spent his own life delving into the questions his father had avoided, including the Resurrection,[88] the Holy Spirit,[89] Elijah as an archetypal image,[90] gnosticism,[91] the Trinity,[92] and symbols of transformation in the Mass.[93] Indeed, Jung believed there was an intrinsic religious instinct in the psyche, at least equal in importance to the other major instincts (creativity, hunger, aggression and sexuality).[94]

Jung found religious images in the individuation material of his patients.[95] Christ, for example, may appear as an image of the archetypal Self,[96] a theme Edward Edinger has developed.[97] One of Jung's most controversial and important statements about religion was his essay "Answer to Job,"[98] which he wrote because he was disturbed about the state of the modern world.[99] In this essay, Jung unfolds a new meaning in the story of Job—that Job became conscious of an unresolved split in the image of God, requiring God to incarnate in his creature man in order to understand his own nature. Edinger has seen this as the chief myth of the present world: man must now help to carry the burden previously placed upon the image of God.[100] As previously mentioned, he identifies Jung as the first exemplar of this new age.

The implications of Jungian theory for religion are revolutionary and have perhaps been ignored for that reason, while Freud, who relegated religion to an "illusion," was easily studied in theological discourse. Theologians are just beginning to deal with Jung, but none as yet has faced the radical implications of his position. One theological discussion of Jung tends to focus only on the unconscious relationship between Freud and Jung, without apprehending the truly challenging questions that Jung poses for religion.[101]

The psyche makes images of God. These can be seen in dreams and are not limited to religious images that the dreamer knows consciously in waking life.[102] This essentially mysterious reference in dream material to the image of God, conceived in both orthodox and unorthodox ways, may point toward the depths of the psyche as the fountainhead of religious imagery. There are many anecdotal accounts of such dreams, and they are not difficult to collect, for they occur with some frequency. But they are not examined as evidence for the origin of religious imagery in the human psyche. Orthodox religion avoids such an approach, which would threaten the primacy of revealed religion and the codification of it in dogma. Scientists equally avoid such considerations, for the generally materialistic framework of science (perhaps once necessary to free it from dogmatic religion before the Renaissance) does not even allow the questions of religion to be asked in a meaningful way.

Jung has been considered a mystic. Based on the dreams from his early life that Jung discusses in his autobiography, I have even heard him called a childhood schizophrenic by a psychiatrist who should know better. But Jung considered himself an empirical scientist and continually insisted that when he spoke of God he was not making metaphysical assertions, but was referring to *an image in the psyche*, which is just as legitimate a study as anything else in the mind. What Jung left unsaid, however, was the obvious position that all statements about God, "revealed" or not, must be statements made by some human person with a human psyche. And Jung understood a great deal about the human psyche.

The development of a religious tradition depends upon the personal religious experience of some individual who is able to put the experience in such form as to attract others to the vision as a true reflection of an unseen reality. An archetypal image that manifests in the life of an individual, if sufficiently integrated and presented to others, accumulates about itself the religious practice of persons in collective consciousness. The archetypal experience gains a "body" of imagery and dogma and is embedded in a religious tradition. While this preserves the archetypal experience, it also sets it against any future new and perhaps more profound embodiment of that archetype, or of other archetypes.

Scientific Implications

As already mentioned, Jung considered himself an empiricist. Although he worked with the tenuous material of the mind, which most scientists avoid, he approached the psyche with as much objectivity as any empirical scientist. It was only in his autobiographical *Memories, Dreams, Reflections* that Jung spoke directly as himself, without regard to the scientific status of his presentation. He wrote this autobiographical work only when pressured to do so by his own dreams. No one outside Jung himself could have induced him to reveal his thoughts so candidly. It is therefore one of the most valuable documents that he produced. In reading it, one gains a sense of Jung's own personal quest—and can verify for oneself the objective and scientific manner in which he attempted to approach the most mysterious experiences of his life.

Jung's original work with the word-association experiment was presented in the acceptable format of scientific investigation at that time.[103] By adding electrical measurements of skin resistance to the essentially psychological inquiry of the experiment, Jung introduced a new approach to psychosomatic medicine. These measurements were also the beginning of polygraph testing (lie detectors). Jung was innovative in trying to apply these techniques to legal investigations.

Even in his deep religious interests, Jung was the empirical scientist. Jung felt that theology was an attempt to describe a transcendent reality that might also be open to scientific investigation,[104] perhaps the same reality that can be seen in dream and imaginal productions reflecting the objective psyche. In this position, Jung stood clearly in the tradition of the founders of the Society for Psychical Research. Indeed, Jung corresponded with J.B. Rhine, the father of parapsychology, hoping that Rhine's laboratory experiments demonstrating extrasensory perception might furnish scientific evidence for realities of the psyche that Jung had observed in his consulting room. Much of the Jung-Rhine correspondence has been included in Jung's published letters.

After a number of searches, both before and after Rhine's death, I was finally able to locate Rhine's folder of correspondence with Jung, which had been misfiled in the papers of Louisa Rhine now in the Duke University Archives. There are a few interesting interchanges between Jung and Rhine that show the latter's strong focus on demonstrable experiments, and the equally strong concern of Jung about the implications of the experimental work for the nature of the psyche. While Rhine is concerned with establishing the experimental facts, Jung is racing ahead to comprehend the meaning of those facts in a larger picture. Both men appear deeply committed to science while profoundly convinced that science can be used to reveal meanings that have traditionally been carried by religious belief. It was largely through the urging of Rhine that Jung published in summary form his own thoughts about parapsychology.[105]

Jung himself attempted an experimental verification of the principle of synchronicity, which is very close to the meaning of psi-phenomena or ESP.[106] The experimental results were uncertain, and could not be replicated in a second experiment, but it is clear that Jung trusted the experimental method to yield important results, even in the unusual phenomena of synchronicity. When accused by Martin Buber of being gnostic, Jung clearly defined himself as a psychiatrist interested in empirical evidence in the service of healing.[107]

Although he showed continued interest in religions of the East, Jung was deeply concerned with the religious tradition of the West and repeatedly cautioned that Western man should not abandon his own empirical foundations. This position again reflects Jung's basic stance as a Western scientist. In the West, alchemy gave rise to science *as well as* secretly preserving an esoteric discipline aimed at self-knowledge, protecting it from repeated collective attempts to impose uniformity of belief. The outer exoteric science that developed from alchemy is of course chemistry, one of the basic modern sciences. We are still concerned with the inner esoteric science of alchemy, which a series of dreams led Jung to recognize as the forerunner of depth psychology.[108]

Jung's work does much to bridge this still unhealed split between science and religion. Standing firmly on his belief in the empirical investigation of a meaningful universe, Jung nevertheless did not hesitate to ask the most probing and difficult questions about the origins and meaning of religious belief. His concept of the archetype, the basic innate tendency of the psyche to form patterns from experience, is relevant to both the phenomenology of religion and to the structuring of scientific concepts.

In his later theoretical views, Jung considered the archetype to be *psychoid*, by which he meant to emphasize that at the limits of our ability to observe it is impossible to determine whether the archetype is pure psyche or is also involved in the structure of matter.[109] "Psychoid" indicates that the archetype may be a principle underlying both the psyche and the world. Evidence for the psychoid nature of the archetype is to be found in both ESP and synchronistic phenomena. The development of creative insights in mathematics also suggests a deep connection between patterns of the mind and patterns in the physical universe, for some new mathematical theories that are developed wholly from the psyche are nevertheless found to be precise representations of the structure of the universe revealed by scientific experiment.[110]

If the nature of the archetype is truly psychoid, then we are living in a very mysterious universe indeed!—one that is quite different, in its depths, from the world of consciousness where subjectivity seems so radically separated from the physical world outside ourselves. It would also mean that in probing the depths of the psyche we are simultaneously approaching an understanding of the physical world.

Jung's profound understanding of the psyche resulted in what is to my mind the most promising model yet developed to bridge the tragic gap between science and religion. Mankind cannot long nor happily endure the present separation of our two views of the universe. The first, science, is lodged in an unnecessarily materialistic framework, while religion, the other great repository of our highest hopes and values, is too often unnecessarily dogmatic or (what is worse and even more dangerous) presented in the guise of secular "isms" that carry unconscious religious fervor. This is one world, one universe, and human values are not pasted on it from outside, but arise from the very depths of the objective psyche, which is as real as the world of external reality. These two are, in fact, one.

We must find our way to a more precise understanding of this unity before the radical separation of science and value writes a tragic chapter in the long emergence of human civilization and culture. Jung is perhaps our most reliable guide in this urgent quest.

Concluding Statement

This volume has been an introduction to the world of Jungian experience. The reader should have a sense of the actual process of Jungian analysis, as well as a beginning understanding of the nature of the psyche, and thus be better able to judge if a personal Jungian analysis is likely to further his or her own individuation.

In addition, I have tried to indicate that the Jungian experience is more profound than personal analysis, for analysis, when successful, is in the service of individuation, the continuing exploration of one's own personal meaning and destiny. The Jungian experience may perhaps be even more profound than the process of individuation, the basic life task of the individual human being. Jung saw deeply into the individual psyche, but also into the mysterious world of the objective psyche which may prove to be the origin of both ourselves and our world. Currents in this collective psyche may foreshadow mass events in the world, just as Jung found premonitions of the First World War in the dreams of his patients. Investigation of this frontier has hardly begun.

Jungian thought is an effective bridge between understanding the individual and articulating the wider concerns of the fate and psychic history of mankind, between empirical scientific investigation and the spontaneous emergence of religious imagery in the psyche. It is a healing force in the world as much as it is a therapeutic approach to neurosis in the individual.

I wish to conclude this book the way it began, with a personal testimonial. I believe the classical Jungian view of the psyche is valid. This belief is based upon my own experience of analysis, for which I am endlessly grateful, and upon the observations permitted me in sharing the inner processes of so many of my analysands.

Jungian analysis is a Way, in the great sense of traditional religious pathways (though not itself a religion). It is also a research tool yielding views of the psyche in its depths that could be obtained in no other manner. Jung has made a major contribution to our world. I am honored to participate in furthering what he began.

Appendix 1

Structural Elements of the Personality

This section is intended as an aid in understanding the classical Jungian model of the psyche and the technical language used in describing it.

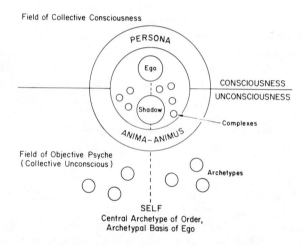

In the above figure the horizontal line represents the division between consciousness (above the line) and the unconscious (below the line). The outer circle defines the personal sphere, within which are the personal elements of the psyche, both conscious and unconscious. Similarly, the area both outside the two circles and above the line indicates contents that are in collective consciousness, and the area both below the line and outside the circles represents contents in the objective psyche (collective unconscious).

In the center of the field of consciousness is the ego complex. Although called a "complex" the ego is unique among complexes. It is based upon the archetype of the Self, the central archetype of order, and is in a sense the representative of the archetypal Self in the field of consciousness. Other complexes that become "attached" to the ego complex also partake of consciousness to some degree. The more they are dissociated from the ego complex the less they are able to enter directly and easily the field of consciousness.

146

When we say "I" we are speaking from the ego complex. We are also tacitly identifying with certain structures associated with the ego, including the body-image and the usual sense of character structure (such as "I am a reliable person"). We also tacitly dwell in other complexes associated with language, grammar, syntax, social (persona) forms and so on. Most of the difficulty of understanding psychopathology, as well as such unusual phenomena as mystical states, hinges upon the ambiguity between the ego complex and "I." My own understanding is that "I" actually refers to the archetypal core of the ego, the Self, which in its pure form is a center of subjectivity with no necessary content. In an observable form, however, the ego complex is always found identified with one or more other complexes, which constitute images of oneself that, in the psychologically naive state, a person takes to be his or her actual identity.

The real identity of the ego complex is the Self. And the identity of the Self is mysterious. It is not entirely unbounded, but it is less bound in time, space and identity than is the naive ego. The Self exists at the level where synchronistic connections are easily possible, but for the ego complex they are always startling and meaningful intrusions from another level of order.

In terms of the Jungian model, the Self is concerned with the process of individuation, both of "itself" and of the situations in which it participates—ultimately the individuation of the universe as one. The naive ego, in contrast, is usually caught in the defense of its images of itself, which from the point of view of the Self are no more important than the various persona roles are for the ego— that is to say, of some importance for given purposes, but ultimately dispensable.

The archetypal Self is conceptually the center of the entire psyche, although it is represented in the diagram as the central structure of the objective psyche, the collective unconscious. It exists as 1) a virtual center of the psyche when perceived by the ego or spoken of in theoretical terms, 2) the archetypal pattern of the ego complex, and 3) a way of speaking about the entire psyche as a unified whole.

The boundary between the ego complex and the outer world of collective consciousness is indicated by the *persona*, a term used for the masks worn in classical Greek drama to amplify the character being portrayed (some masks actually had megaphones built into them to amplify the voice of the actor) and to hide the personal

quality of the actor which might otherwise interfere with the enactment of his role. In psychological usage, persona refers to roles one
plays in relation to other people. Persona refers to much the same
thing as role theory does in sociology, although the persona points
to the actual form of the role that a given person might enact, not
the generalizations of sociological discussion.

The persona is actually multiple, since each person plays many
roles: the father, the physician, the son, the friend, the lover, etc.
In a healthy person, the roles are more or less compatible, although
there is always some dissonance between them. A standard comedy
character is the business tycoon who is henpecked by his wife. In
"Amos and Andy," a now defunct radio program remembered by
many with warm pleasure, this was expressed in a particularly
memorable line: "The Grand High Exalted Omnipotent Master of
the Lodge done got beat up by his wife!"

If the persona is well suited to the individual, it facilitates most
of the impersonal transactions that comprise daily life. Without a
reasonably well-developed persona, a person has a "thin skin" and
the ego feels threatened in even ordinary social interactions. A
persona that is too "thick" hides the ego rather than enhancing its
effectiveness in the world. A particularly common and often tragic
situation is *identification with the persona*, when the ego mistakenly
believes it is nothing but the persona role. Things that threaten the
persona then seem to be threats to the integrity of the ego itself.
Finally, in one who has glimpsed beyond the persona but drawn
back, there is a defensive condition called *regressive restoration of
the persona*—settling for a seemingly secure role, though below
one's potential, rather than face the uncertainties of individuation.

The persona, like all contents of the personal sphere, is comprised
of complexes. It is important to remember that it is the use to which
the complexes are put, not their existence, that can cause difficulty.
The same complex, at different times and under different circumstances, may manifest through the persona, the ego or the
shadow. It might even be projected onto another person toward
whom one then feels all the emotions associated with that complex.

Just as the persona is the interface between the ego and the outer
world, the interface with the inner world is carried by the *anima* (a
feminine figure in the mind of a man) or the *animus* (the corresponding masculine figure in the mind of a woman). These are empirical
concepts, derived largely from Jung's observations of dreams and

fantasy material. In their healthy form they enlarge the personal sphere of the ego through fascination with inner images or some outer task, as well as through involvement with a person of the opposite sex. In their negative or neurotic forms, the anima and animus function as guardian of the presumed "true self"—which is actually a neurotically determined false ego-image. The stronger and more subtle the defenses, the harder it is for the ego to see how it is shielding itself from life.

In recognizing these structural elements of the psyche within oneself, it is important not to define them too tightly. One can all too easily have a concept or thought about oneself, rather than the actual transforming experience of oneself in relation to the unconscious. The ego would seem to be the most easily recognized, since it carries the signature of "I." But anything that establishes a connection with consciousness can speak through "I"—and feel, at least momentarily, as if it were the true ego.

Attention to shifts in emotional tone and the content of what is said or thought are major guides to identifying these parts of one's personality. Experience of the persona is often conscious and carries an "optional" quality: one can choose to behave in a way deemed appropriate to a given situation—that is, express oneself through a persona role. If the persona is not pathological, it is like a suit of clothes and can be donned or removed according to what is proper for the occasion. The shadow arouses anxiety lest it become too conscious or too evident to others, even if the ego is conscious of it subjectively. It feels inferior, as if one were slipping into a less integrated state (although this may also carry fascination).

The shadow can usually be noted in a person of the same sex that one somehow, perhaps irrationally, doesn't like. This is different from disliking a person for actual dislikable qualities—in that case, one simply doesn't like the person but is not troubled by that fact. The person onto whom the shadow is projected rankles one, seeming more important than his or her actual place in one's life. In some cases, this quality of the shadow shades over into the anima or animus and it may be difficult to distinguish these elements.

In projected form, the anima or animus usually falls on a person of the opposite sex, although that maxim has exceptions, particularly if the sexual identity of the ego is confused. Most often the projection is positive, at least initially. With a trained eye, it is sometimes possible to see something of what the projection is about.

It may represent a recurrent neurotic pattern, or there may be positive qualities in the other person that are almost totally unconscious in the person making the projection. It is not unusual in a developing relationship for the positive projection to be mutual, but this is often followed by a defensive negative form when actual relationship over time is attempted, particularly if either or both partners have severe neurotic conflicts. In general, when another person does not "live up to" our expectations, we can be pretty sure that a complex of our own has been projected onto that person.

These are the structural aspects of the personal sphere that are most accessible to introspection and intuition. At times they are shown in fine detail in dreams, and even the relationships between them may be seen in some dreams. It is well to remember that all complexes have an archetypal core, so that in the experience of these structural components, and other complexes, one is also experiencing the archetypes. Most archetypal meanings are mediated through the personal sphere, acquiring color from those structures. Only rarely does an archetypal experience come with such force that it brings into the personal sphere a sense of the numinosity, fascination and power of the archetype.

Some drugs produce fairly raw experiences of archetypal themes, either because the normal ego structure is chemically impaired by the drug or because the usual level of consciousness is lowered. Highly stressful events, such as the birth of a child or the death of someone close, can evoke a sense of archetypal meaning showing through the usual mundane veneer of life. Some religious and meditative experiences carry an archetypal numinosity. At times of collective crisis people seem more prone to experience events with an archetypal tone.

The deliberate study of "archetypal" material, as in the academic study of symbolism, dividing experiences into various categories named for different "gods," etc., is a pale substitute for a genuine archetypal experience arising from the depths of one's own psyche. No one who has experienced the actual numinosity of an archetypal event can confuse that with the consciously cultivated facsimile. An integrated understanding of the impersonal, archetypal realm is only acquired through prolonged reflection on one's personal experience of the complexes.

Appendix 2

How and Where to Find Jungian Analysts

Although there has been a great increase in the number of certified Jungian analysts in the last decade, they are still few and far between. Every graduate analyst has a directory of members of the International Association for Analytical Psychology. The current directory lists some 800 English-speaking analysts, of which about half are in the United States.

One of the best ways to locate a qualified Jungian analyst is to ask someone who has had such an analysis. Alternatively, the local county or state medical society or psychological association is often aware of specialized practitioners in a particular area, even if they are not members of those professional associations.

There are at present seven American Jung societies with training programs. In addition to their own members, they can provide information on Jungian analysts practicing in other areas. Analysis may also be available from training candidates at a reduced fee. The current addresses and phone numbers of these societies, east to west, are as follows:

C.G. Jung Foundation for Analytical Psychology
28 East 39th Street, New York, NY 10016
Telephone (212) 697-6430.

New England Society of Jungian Analysts
264 Beacon Street, Boston, MA 02116
Telephone (617) 267-5984.

C.G. Jung Institute of Chicago
550 Callan Avenue, Evanston, IL 60202
Telephone (312) 475-4848.

C.G. Jung Institute of San Francisco
2040 Gough Street, San Francisco, CA 94109
Telephone (415) 771-8055.

C.G. Jung Institute of Los Angeles
10349 West Pico Boulevard, Los Angeles, CA 90064
Telephone (213) 556-1193.

Society of Jungian Analysts of San Diego
3525 Front St., San Diego, CA 92103
Telephone (619) 291-JUNG.

Inter-Regional Society of Jungian Analysts
Contact: Joan Buresch, President
1520 Cerro Gordo, Santa Fe, NM 87501
Telephone (505) 988-1529.

Although the Inter-Regional Society has no geographical head-quarters, there are major groupings of member analysts in Dallas, Houston and Austin, Texas; Santa Fe, New Mexico; Birmingham, Alabama; Denver and Boulder, Colorado; Minneapolis and St. Paul, Minnesota; Seattle, Washington; Portland, Oregon; and Toronto and Montreal, Canada. There are smaller groupings and individual analysts in many other cities.

In addition to the professional training centers listed above, there are well over a hundred Jungian clubs and societies in North America that sponsor lectures and workshops by Jungian analysts. Most also maintain Jungian-oriented libraries and bookstores. An up-to-date listing of these groups and a calendar of events appears three times a year in the newsletter *In Touch*, published by The Centerpoint Foundation, 33 Main St., Suite 302, Nashua, NH 03060; telephone (603) 880-3020.

Appendix 3

Suggested Readings

The best sources of Jungian thought are of course the writings of Jung himself, most of which are published in the twenty-volume *Collected Works* (CW). Many of the individual volumes are now available in paperback editions. A complete list of topics covered in the *Collected Works* appears at the back of each volume. Volumes 19 and 20 are a general bibliography and a general index.

A good starting point is *Two Essays on Analytical Psychology* (CW 7), an excellent theoretical presentation of Jung's views, including material on typology and anima/animus. Also, the section of "Definitions" in *Psychological Types* (CW 6) gives clear, concise explanations of the major terms used in Jungian discourse.

Although excluded from the *Collected Works* at Jung's request, his autobiographical *Memories, Dreams, Reflections* (New York: Pantheon Books, 1963) is in many ways the most interesting material he wrote, showing his own quest for the meaning of his life and work. Joseph Campbell presents a good chronological selection of Jung's writings in *The Portable Jung* (New York: Viking Press, 1971). A classic and valuable introduction to Jung's work, arranged according to topic, is *Complex/Archetype/Symbol* by Jolande Jacobi (Princeton: Princeton University Press, 1959). William McGuire and R.F.C. Hull edited *C.G. Jung Speaking* (Princeton: Princeton University Press, 1977), a record of interviews and encounters with Jung.

The most authoritative biographies of Jung are by Marie-Louise von Franz, *C.G. Jung: His Myth in Our Time* (New York: Putnam's, 1975) and Barbara Hannah, *C.G. Jung: A Biographical Memoir* (New York: Putnam's, 1976). They both worked closely with Jung, especially during the years of the Second World War and afterward until his death. Von Franz's biography deals more with the meaning of Jung's work, while Hannah's book is rich in personal details. Another quite readable narrative of Jung's life is Laurens van der Post's *Jung and the Story of Our Time* (New York: Pantheon, 1975).

Three overviews of Jungian dream interpretation are available:

Applied Dream Analysis (Washington: Winston, 1978) by Mary Ann Mattoon, and two by myself, *Clinical Uses of Dreams: Jungian Interpretations and Enactments* (New York: Grune and Stratton, 1977) and the more condensed *Jungian Dream Interpretation: A Handbook of Theory and Practice*, in the same Inner City series as the present volume.

All titles in the Inner City series, started in 1980 "to promote the understanding and practical application" of Jung's work, are by Jungian analysts. Those by Marie-Louise von Franz, edited from transcriptions of her lectures in English, give a particularly lucid view of Jung's own position: *The Psychological Meaning of Redemption Motifs in Fairytales, On Divination and Synchronicity: The Psychological Meaning of Chance* and *Alchemy: An Introduction to the Symbolism and the Psychology*. (A complete listing of Inner City titles, with brief descriptions, appears at the end of this volume.)

A number of von Franz's earlier lectures have also been published by Spring Publications, including *Creation Myths, Individuation in Fairy Tales, An Introduction to the Interpretation of Fairy Tales, Problems of the Feminine in Fairy Tales* and *Shadow and Evil in Fairy Tales*. Her definitive discussion of the syndrome of the *puer aeternus* (originally published by Spring Publications in 1970) is now available in a revised edition as *Puer Aeternus: The Adult Struggle with the Paradise of Childhood* (Santa Monica: Sigo Press, 1981).

Practicing psychotherapists will benefit particularly from *Jungian Analysis*, edited by Murray Stein, published in hardcover by Open Court and in paperback by Shambhala Press. It contains chapters by a number of practicing Jungian analysts, including myself, that present a comprehensive view of the current status of Jungian analysis in the United States. The unique British school of Jungian analysis, influenced by Melanie Klein and the object relations school of Freudian psychoanalysis, is well represented in *The Library of Analytical Psychology*, a series published for the Society of Analytical Psychology by Academic Press; this series is edited by Michael Fordham, Rosemary Gordon, Judith Hubback and Kenneth Lambert, all of whom have contributed to it as well.

An excellent general introduction to Jungian analysis is Edward C. Whitmont's classic *The Symbolic Quest* (New York: Putnam's, 1969). One of the best views of psychosis from a Jungian perspective is John Weir Perry's *Roots of Renewal in Myth and Madness* (San Francisco: Josey-Bass, 1976). The C.G. Jung Educational Center of Houston has published Jane Wheelwright's study of the animus, *For Women Growing Older*, edited by Jungian analyst Martha Shelton Wolf.

The different "schools" of Jungian analysis are discussed by Andrew Samuels in *Jung and the Post-Jungians* (London: Routledge and Kegan Paul, 1985). This is a useful survey, although to my mind Samuels gives rather more prominence to "archetypal psychology" than it warrants, including in that variant of Jungian analysis authors who are not trained Jungian analysts (which he does not do with the classical and the developmental schools). Archetypal psychology grew largely out of the work of James Hillman, one-time director of studies at the Zurich Institute, and is best sampled in his *Revisioning Psychology* or in the journal *Spring* which he edits.

A highly respected—and the first—periodical in the field of Jungian psychology is the *Journal of Analytical Psychology*, published in London under the editorship of Rosemary Gordon. *Quadrant,* a journal published by the C.G. Jung Foundation of New York, has expanded in recent years and is an important arena for discussion of developing trends in Jungian psychology. It is edited by a distinguished board, chaired by Maurice Krasnow. Another important publication, with extensive reviews of books and films relevant to Jungian psychology is *The San Francisco Jung Institute Library Journal,* edited by John Beebe. The Los Angeles Institute publishes *Psychological Perspectives,* until recently edited by William Walcott, which presents a more popular, somewhat literary view of Jungian psychology, although the emphasis may change under the newly appointed editor, Ernest Rossi.

A new and much-needed journal devoted to the clinical practice of Jungian analysis is *Chiron,* named for the mythical centaur who was the teacher of Asclepius. It is published by Chiron Press through the Chicago Jung Institute and is edited by Murray Stein and Nathan Schwartz-Salant. *Chiron* has published papers of the annual Ghost Ranch conferences, which are held in New Mexico and are open to Jungian analysts, candidates and, as space permits, to a limited number of others. In addition to *Chiron*, Chiron Press has begun publication of a series of books oriented toward the clinical practice of analytical psychology.

Special mention must be given here to the remarkable ten-hour film documentary *The Way of the Dream*, featuring Marie-Louise von Franz interpreting dreams told on camera by the dreamers themselves. *The Way of the Dream* was produced by Windrose Films, Toronto, and directed by Jungian analyst Fraser Boa. Since 1985 it has been presented in special weekend showings throughout North America, but will eventually be on public television and available in video cassette form. It is also expected that a transcript will be published.

The Jungian literature grows at an accelerating pace. These few suggestions are meant only as an appetizer, to permit easy entry into this complex and intricate field.

Notes

CW—*The Collected Works of C.G. Jung,* 20 vols., trans. R.F.C. Hull, ed. H. Read, M. Fordham, G. Adler, Wm. McGuire, Bollingen Series XX (Princeton: Princeton University Press, 1953-1979).

1. *Memories, Dreams, Reflections,* trans. Richard and Clara Winston, ed. Aniela Jaffé (New York: Pantheon Books, 1963), p. 308.

2. Perhaps the best known work on the psychology of the puer is Marie-Louise von Franz, *Puer Aeternus: The Adult Struggle with the Paradise of Childhood,* 2nd ed. (Santa Monica: Sigo Press, 1981); see also Daryl Sharp, *The Secret Raven: Conflict and Transformation* (Toronto: Inner City Books, 1980).

3. See Jung, "Definitions," *Psychological Types,* CW 6, pars. 708-709.

4. The experience of the archetypal Self, in terms of the biblical story of Job, is graphically presented in Edward F. Edinger, *Encounter with the Self: A Jungian Commentary on William Blake's Illustrations of the Book of Job* (Toronto: Inner City Books, 1986).

5. *C.G. Jung Letters,* vol. 1, trans. R.F.C. Hull, ed. Gerhard Adler and Aniela Jaffé, Bollingen Series XCV (Princeton: Princeton University Press, 1974), pp. 166-172.

6. See James A. Hall, "Jung and Hillman: Implications for a Psychology of Religion," in *Jung and the Study of Religion,* ed. L.H. Martin and J. Goss (New York: American Universities Press, 1986).

7. Edinger, *The Creation of Consciousness: Jung's Myth for Modern Man* (Toronto: Inner City Books, 1984), pp. 12-13.

8. Roy Laurens, *Fully Alive* (Dallas: Saybrook Press, 1985).

9. Samuels, *Jung and the Post-Jungians* (London: Routledge and Kegan Paul, 1985).

10. See Jung, "The Psychology of the Transference," *The Practice of Psychotherapy,* CW 16; see also Mario Jacoby, *The Analytic Encounter: Transference and Human Relationship* (Toronto: Inner City Books, 1984), pp. 25-28.

11. *C.G. Jung Letters,* vol. 2, pp. 217-221. Jung's colleague Marie-Louise von Franz also questions the value of group therapy; see "On Group Psychology," *Quadrant,* vol. 13 (1973).

12. Jung, "Commentary on 'The Secret of the Golden Flower,'" *Alchemical Studies,* CW 13, par. 4.

13. Jung, "Synchronicity: An Acausal Connecting Principle," *The Structure and Dynamics of the Psyche,* CW 8.

14. See James A. Hall, *Clinical Uses of Dreams: Jungian Interpretations and Enactments* (New York: Grune and Stratton, 1977), pp. 141-182.

15. See Jung, *Experimental Researches,* CW 2, Part 1: "Studies in Word Association."

16. Jung, "The Psychology of Dementia Praecox," *The Psychogenesis of Mental Disease,* CW 3, par. 86 and note 9.

17. See Hall, *Clinical Uses of Dreams,* pp. 172-173, and *Jungian Dream Interpretation: A Handbook of Theory and Practice* (Toronto: Inner City Books, 1983), pp. 28-33.

18. See M. Polanyi, *Personal Knowledge: Toward a Post-Critical Philosophy* (Chicago: University of Chicago Press, 1958).

19. I have written about this at length in *Clinical Uses of Dreams* (particularly chapter 7) and in a condensed form in *Jungian Dream Interpretation,* pp. 109-111.

20. *Journal of the American Society of Clinical Hypnosis,* vol. 26 (1984), pp. 159-165.

21. See Victor W. Turner, *The Ritual Process* (Chicago: Aldine Publishing Co., 1969).

22. D.W. Winnicott, *Collected Papers* (London: Tavistock, 1958).

23. Jung, *Two Essays on Analytical Psychology,* CW 7, pars. 254-259, 471-475.

24. Edward F. Edinger, *Ego and Archetype: Individuation and the Religious Function of the Psyche* (New York: Putnam's, 1972), pp. 5-6.

25. Personal communication.

26. Jung, "Psychology and Religion," *Psychology and Religion: West and East,* CW 11, par. 139.

27. I have been impressed by the work of the Japanese Buddhist scholar Nishitani (see *Religion and Nothingness,* trans. J. van Bragt; Los Angeles: University of California Press, 1982), whose concept of *sunyata* or emptiness is quite suggestive of the Jungian objective psyche, as an indescribable field of possibilities out of which the world is constituted.

28. Jung, "The Psychology of the Child Archetype," *The Archetypes and the Collective Unconscious,* CW 9i, par. 271.

29. See Jung, "Definitions," *Psychological Types,* CW 6, pars. 808-811.

30. See F. Alexander and S. Selesnik, *The History of Psychiatry* (New York: Harper and Row, 1966), pp. 221, 262-265, 294-295, 376.

31. See Sharp, *The Secret Raven,* pp. 75-82.

32. Von Franz's study of the puer (see above, note 2) is based on a close psychological interpretation of *The Little Prince.*

33. June Singer and Mary Loomis, *The Singer-Loomis Inventory of Personality* (Palo Alto: Consulting Psychologists Press, 1984).

34. See, for instance, M. Mahler, K.F. Pine and A. Bergman, *The Psychological Birth of the Human Infant* (New York: Basic Books, 1975).

35. See John W. Perry, *Roots of Renewal in Myth and Madness* (San Francisco: Jossey-Bass, 1976).

36. Edinger, *Ego and Archetype,* p. 41; see also Aldo Carotenuto, *The Spiral Way: A Woman's Healing Journey* (Toronto: Inner City Books, 1986).

37. See Jung, "The Problem of the Attitude-Type," *Two Essays on Analytical Psychology,* CW 7.

38. Ibid., par. 62; see also *Psychological Types,* CW 6, par. 4.

39. Jung, "General Description of the Types," ibid., pars. 330-671.

40. My own analytical work is done primarily face to face with the patient, although my psychiatric training included treating some control cases on the couch. In hypnoanalytic work I offer the analysand the choice of lying on a couch or sitting in a reclining chair with an ottoman. Since dream interpretation is my own preferred method of following the patient's process (including T/CT questions), I have never been stirred by arguments for or against the use of the couch. Lying on a couch clearly promotes more dissociation in the analysand (as does hypnotherapy) and is one way of inducing a more regressed state—if that is desired.

41. The question of analytic fees is also discussed in Jacoby, *The Analytic Encounter,* pp. 93-98.

42. The work of R.D. Langs is well presented in *The Therapeutic Interaction,* 2 vols. (New York: Jason Aransch, 1976).

43. See Nathan Schwartz-Salant, "Archetypal Factors Underlying Sexual Acting-Out in the Transference/Countertransference," *Chiron 1* (1984). See also Jacoby, *The Analytic Encounter,* chapter 7, "Erotic Love in Analysis."

44. I am indebted to my colleague Gladys Guy Brown, friend and

co-therapist in group work for many years, for assistance in defining the analysand's area of responsibility.

45. Jung, "The Psychology of the Transference," *The Practice of Psychotherapy*, CW 16, par. 422.

46. The alchemical drawings used by Jung in "The Psychology of the Transference" are from illustrations for a text by Gerhard Dorn. For a more complete compilation of these see A. McLean, *The Rosary of the Philosophers* (Edinburgh: Magnum Opus Hermetic Sourceworks, 1980).

47. See Jung, "Problems of Modern Psychotherapy," *The Practice of Psychotherapy*, CW 16, pars. 53-75.

48. Jung, "The Psychology of Dementia Praecox," *The Psychogenesis of Mental Disease*, CW 3, par. 195.

49. Jung, "On the Psychogenesis of Schizophrenia," ibid., par. 531.

50. Jung, "Definitions," *Psychological Types*, CW 6, par. 828; see also Jung, "The Transcendent Function," *The Structure and Dynamics of the Psyche*, CW 8.

51. M. Miyuki, "Self-Realization in the Ten Ox-Herding Pictures," in *Buddhism and Jungian Psychology*, ed. J.F. Spiegelman and M. Miyuki (Phoenix: Falcon Press, 1985).

52. See R.J. White, *The Interpretation of Dreams: Oneirocritica by Artemidorus* (Park Ridge, NJ: Noyes Press, 1975).

53. Jung's approach to dreams is presented most extensively in "General Aspects of Dream Psychology," and "On the Nature of Dreams," both in *The Structure and Dynamics of the Psyche*, CW 8.

54. See, for example, Hall, *Clinical Uses of Dreams*, pp. 266-271.

55. See Hall, "Religious Images in Dreams," *Journal of Religion and Health*, vol. 18 (1979), and "Religious Symbols in Dreams of Analytical Patients," *Journal of the American Academy of Psychoanalysis*, vol. 9 (1981).

56. R.B. Onians, *The Origins of European Thought* (New York: Arno Press, 1973).

57. See above, note 16.

58. Jung, "On the Nature of Dreams," *The Structure and Dynamics of the Psyche*, CW 8, pars. 545ff.

59. See Jung, "Introduction to Wickes' *Analyse der Kinderseele*," [The Inner World of Childhood] *The Development of Personality*, CW 17, pars. 93-97, and "Child Development and Education," ibid., pars. 106f.

60. See Hall, *Clinical Uses of Dreams*, p. 335.

61. See H.B. Crasilneck and James A. Hall, *Clinical Hypnosis: Principles and Applications,* 2nd ed. (New York: Grune and Stratton, 1985).

62. See Edward Whitmont, "Group Therapy and Analytical Psychology," *Journal of Analytical Psychology,* vol. 9, no. 1 (January 1964).

63. Jung, "The Psychology of the Transference," *The Practice of Psychotherapy,* CW 16, par. 433.

64. Jung, "Marriage as a Psychological Relationship," *The Development of Personality,* CW 17, par. 327.

65. Ibid., par. 331c. For a particularly original and creative presentation of how to deal with anima/animus interaction in couple therapy, see Polly Young-Eisendrath, *Hags and Heroes: A Feminist Approach to Jungian Psychotherapy with Couples* (Toronto: Inner City Books, 1984).

66. Jung, "The Family Constellation," *Experimental Researches,* CW 2, pars. 999-1014.

67. Jung, "Psychic Conflicts in a Child," *The Development of Personality,* CW 17.

68. Jung, "Symbols and the Interpretation of Dreams," *The Symbolic Life,* CW 18, par. 492.

69. "Some Crucial Points in Psychoanalysis: A Correspondence between Dr. Jung and Dr. Loÿ," *Freud and Psychoanalysis,* CW 4, par. 601.

70. Jung, "Symbols and the Interpretation of Dreams," *The Symbolic Life,* CW 18, par. 492.

71. Crasilneck and Hall, *Clinical Hypnosis,* pp. 36-41.

72. See John Watkins, *The Therapeutic Self* (New York: Human Sciences Press, 1978).

73. This is the overall message of Jung's correspondence with Dr. Loÿ; see above, note 69.

74. Edinger, *The Creation of Consciousness,* chapter 1, "The New Myth."

75. Jung, *Memories, Dreams, Reflections,* pp. 196-197; for an outline of yoga theory and practice in relation to the development of Jung's thought, see Harold Coward, *Jung and Eastern Thought* (Albany: State University Press of New York; 1985).

76. T.S. Eliot, "Burnt Norton," lines 62-67.

77. See, for instance, H. Kaplan, "History of Psychosomatic Medicine," in *Comprehensive Textbook of Psychiatry,* ed. H. Kaplan, A. Freedman and B. Sadock (Baltimore: Williams and Wilkins,

1980), vol. 1, pp. 1843-1853, and P.A. Knapp, "Current Theoretical Concepts in Psychosomatic Medicine," ibid., pp. 1853-1862.

78. T.S. Eliot, "Little Gidding," lines 239-243.

79. Ibid., lines 253-254.

80. "The 'Face to Face' Interview," *C.G. Jung Speaking,* Bollingen Series XCVII, ed. W. McGuire and R.F.C. Hull (Princeton: Princeton University Press, 1977), p. 438.

81. See Jung, "The Soul and Death," *The Structure and Dynamics of the Psyche,* CW 8.

82. F.W.H. Myers, *Human Personality and Its Survival of Bodily Death* (New York: Garrett Publications, 1954).

83. Jung, *Memories, Dreams, Reflections,* p. 325.

84. Ibid., p. 313.

85. Freud's theories of the ego, superego and id are outlined in his *New Introductory Lectures on Psycho-Analysis and Other Works* (London: Hogarth Press, 1964).

86. David Bakan, *Sigmund Freud and the Jewish Mystical Tradition* (Boston: Beacon Press, 1958).

87. Jung, *Memories, Dreams, Reflections,* pp. 53-56.

88. "On Resurrection," *The Symbolic Life,* CW 18, pars. 1558-1574.

89. "Letter to Père Lachat," ibid., pars. 1532-1557.

90. "Letter to Père Bruno," ibid., pars. 1518-1531.

91. "Gnostic Symbols of the Self," *Aion,* CW 9ii, pars. 287-346.

92. "A Psychological Approach to the Dogma of the Trinity," *Psychology and Religion: West and East,* CW 11, pars. 108-296.

93. "Transformation Symbolism in the Mass," ibid., pars. 202-296.

94. Jung, "The Undiscovered Self," *Civilization in Transition,* CW 10, par. 512; see also "Psychological Factors in Human Behaviour," *The Structure and Dynamics of the Human Psyche,* CW 8, pars. 237-245, where the religious attitude is seen as deriving from the reflective instinct.

95. See "A Study in the Process of Individuation," and "Concerning Mandala Symbolism," *The Archetypes and the Collective Unconscious,* CW 9i.

96. "Jung and Religious Belief," *The Symbolic Life,* CW 18, pars. 1650ff.

97. Edinger, *Ego and Archetype,* passim.

98. "Answer to Job," *Psychology and Religion,* CW 11, pars. 553-758.

99. "Concerning 'Answer to Job,'" *The Symbolic Life,* CW 18, par. 1498a.

100. Edinger, *The Creation of Consciousness,* esp. chapter 3, "Depth Psychology as the New Dispensation: Reflections on Jung's 'Answer to Job.'"

101. See P. Homans, *Jung in Context* (Chicago: Chicago University Press, 1982). Homans is a scholar, not a clinician, and shows some fundamental misunderstandings about Jungian theory as it is actually applied. More explicit in dealing with the theological issues, though again not clinically oriented, is John P. Dourley, *The Illness That We Are: A Jungian Critique of Christianity* (Toronto: Inner City Books, 1984). Dourley is a Jungian analyst, Catholic priest and professor of religious studies.

102. See above, note 55. I also deal with these issues in "Psychiatry and Religion: A Review and Projection of Future Needs," *Anglican Theological Review,* vol. 63 (1981); "The Work of J.B. Rhine: Implications for Religion," *Journal of Parapsychology,* vol. 45 (1981); "Jungian Concepts in Religious Counseling," *Perkins Journal,* vol. 36 (1982); and "A Jungian Perspective on Parapsychology: Implications for Science and Religion," paper presented at the Parapsychology Foundation Conference, Rome, 1985.

     Jung refers to "how the unconscious of Protestants behaves when it has to compensate an intensely religious attitude." ("Foreward to Froboese-Thiele: *Traüme—Eine Quelle Religiöser Erfarhrung?* [Dreams—A Source of Religious Experience?]," *The Symbolic Life,* CW 18, par. 1581.

103. See above, note 15.

104. See above, note 89.

105. *C.G. Jung Letters,* vol. 1, pp. 393-395.

106. See "Synchronicity: An Acausal Connecting Principle," chapter 2, "An Astrological Experiment," *The Structure and Dynamics of the Psyche,* CW 8, pars. 872-915. A condensed version appears in *The Symbolic Life,* CW 18, pars. 1174-1192.

107. "Religion and Psychology: A Reply to Martin Buber," ibid., pars. 1499-1513.

108. See *Memories, Dreams, Reflections,* chapter 7, "The Work."

109. "On the Nature of the Psyche," *The Structure and Dynamics of the Psyche,* CW 8, pars. 417ff.

110. See Gary Zukov, *The Dancing Wu Li Masters: An Overview of the New Physics* (New York: Bantam Books, 1980).

Glossary of Jungian Terms

Anima (Latin, "soul"). The unconscious, feminine side of a man's personality. She is personified in dreams by images of women ranging from prostitute and seductress to spiritual guide (Wisdom). She is the eros principle, hence a man's anima development is reflected in how he relates to women. Identification with the anima can appear as moodiness, effeminacy, and oversensitivity. Jung calls the anima *the archetype of life itself.*

Animus (Latin, "spirit"). The unconscious, masculine side of a woman's personality. He personifies the logos principle. Identification with the animus can cause a woman to become rigid, opinionated, and argumentative. More positively, he is the inner man who acts as a bridge between the woman's ego and her own creative resources in the unconscious.

Archetypes. Irrepresentable in themselves, but their effects appear in consciousness as the archetypal images and ideas. These are universal patterns or motifs which come from the collective unconscious and are the basic content of religions, mythologies, legends, and fairytales. They emerge in individuals through dreams and visions.

Association. A spontaneous flow of interconnected thoughts and images around a specific idea, determined by unconscious connections.

Complex. An emotionally charged group of ideas or images. At the "center" of a complex is an archetype or archetypal image.

Constellate. Whenever there is a strong emotional reaction to a person or a situation, a complex has been constellated (activated).

Ego. The central complex in the field of consciousness. A strong ego can relate objectively to activated contents of the unconscious (i.e., other complexes), rather than identifying with them, which appears as a state of possession.

Feeling. One of the four psychic functions. It is a rational function which evaluates the worth of relationships and situations. Feeling must be distinguished from emotion, which is due to an activated complex.

Individuation. The conscious realization of one's unique psychological reality, including both strengths and limitations. It leads to the experience of the Self as the regulating center of the psyche.

Inflation. A state in which one has an unrealistically high or low (negative inflation) sense of identity. It indicates a regression of consciousness into unconsciousness, which typically happens when the ego takes too many unconscious contents upon itself and loses the faculty of discrimination.

Intuition. One of the four psychic functions. It is the irrational function which tells us the possibilities inherent in the present. In contrast to sensation (the function which perceives immediate reality through the physical senses) intuition perceives via the unconscious, e.g., flashes of insight of unknown origin.

Participation mystique. A term derived from the anthropologist Lévy-Bruhl, denoting a primitive, psychological connection with objects, or between persons, resulting in a strong unconscious bond.

Persona (Latin, "actor's mask"). One's social role, derived from the expectations of society and early training. A strong ego relates to the outside world through a flexible persona; identification with a specific persona (doctor, scholar, artist, etc.) inhibits psychological development.

Projection. The process whereby an unconscious quality or characteristic of one's own is perceived and reacted to in an outer object or person. Projection of the anima or animus onto a real women or man is experienced as falling in love. Frustrated expectations indicate the need to withdraw projections, in order to relate to the reality of other people.

Puer aeternus (Latin, "eternal youth"). Indicates a certain type of man who remains too long in adolescent psychology, generally associated with a strong unconscious attachment to the mother (actual or symbolic). Positive traits are spontaneity and openness to change. His female counterpart is the **puella,** an "eternal girl" with a corresponding attachment to the father-world.

Self. The archetype of wholeness and the regulating center of the personality. It is experienced as a transpersonal power which transcends the ego, e.g., God.

Senex (Latin, "old man"). Associated with attitudes that come with advancing age. Negatively, this can mean cynicism, rigidity and extreme conservatism; positive traits are responsibility, orderliness and self-discipline. A well-balanced personality functions appropriately within the puer-senex polarity.

Shadow. An unconscious part of the personality characterized by traits and attitudes, whether negative or positive, which the conscious ego tends to reject or ignore. It is personified in dreams by persons of the same sex as the dreamer. Consciously assimilating one's shadow usually results in an increase of energy.

Symbol. The best possible expression for something essentially unknown. Symbolic thinking is non-linear, right-brain oriented; it is complementary to logical, linear, left-brain thinking.

Transcendent function. The reconciling "third" which emerges from the unconscious (in the form of a symbol or a new attitude) after the conflicting opposites have been consciously differentiated, and the tension between them held.

Transference and countertransference. Particular cases of projection, commonly used to describe the unconscious, emotional bonds that arise between two persons in an analytic or therapeutic relationship.

Uroboros. The mythical snake or dragon that eats its own tail. It is a symbol both for individuation as a self-contained, circular process, and for narcissistic self-absorption.

Index

Studies in Jungian Psychology
by Jungian Analysts

LIMITED EDITION PAPERBACKS

Prices quoted are in U.S. dollars (except for Canadian orders)

1. The Secret Raven: Conflict and Transformation.
Daryl Sharp (Toronto). ISBN 0-919123-00-7. 128 pp. $10
A practical study of *puer aeternus* psychology, with special attention to dream interpretation, the provisional life, relationships, mid-life crisis, the mother complex and Jung's concepts of anima and shadow. Illustrated.

2. The Psychological Meaning of Redemption Motifs in Fairytales.
Marie-Louise von Franz (Zurich). ISBN 0-919123-01-5. 128 pp. $10
A unique account of the significance of fairytales for an understanding of individuation. Particularly helpful for its symbolic approach to the meaning of typical dream motifs (bathing, beating, clothes, animals, etc.).

3. On Divination and Synchronicity:
The Psychology of Meaningful Chance.
Marie-Louise von Franz (Zurich). ISBN 0-919123-02-3. 128 pp. $10
A penetrating study of the meaning of time, number and methods of divining fate such as the I Ching and astrology, contrasting Western scientific ideas with those of the Chinese and so-called primitives. Illustrated.

4. The Owl Was a Baker's Daughter:
Obesity, Anorexia Nervosa and the Repressed Feminine.
Marion Woodman (Toronto). ISBN 0-919123-03-1. 144 pp. $10
A modern classic in feminine psychology, with particular attention to the body as mirror of the psyche in eating disorders and weight disturbances. Explores the personal and cultural loss of the feminine principle, through case studies, dreams, Christianity and mythology. Illustrated.

5. Alchemy: Introduction to the Symbolism and the Psychology.
Marie-Louise von Franz (Zurich). ISBN 0-919123-04-X. 288 pp. $16
A detailed guide to what the alchemists were really looking for: emotional balance and wholeness. Invaluable for interpreting images and motifs in modern dreams. Completely demystifies the subject. **84 Illustrations.**

6. Descent to the Goddess. A Way of Initiation for Women.
Sylvia Brinton Perera (New York). ISBN 0-919123-05-8. 112 pp. $10
A timely and provocative study of the need for an inner, female authority in a masculine-oriented society. Based on the Sumerian goddess Inanna-Ishtar's journey to the underworld, her transformation and her return. Rich in insights from dreams, mythology and analysis. (See also title 23)

7. The Psyche as Sacrament: C.G. Jung and Paul Tillich.
John P. Dourley (Ottawa). ISBN 0-919123-06-6. 128 pp. $10
A comparative study from a dual perspective (author is Catholic priest and Jungian analyst), examining the psychological meaning of God, Christ, the Trinity, the Spirit, morality and religion. (See also title 17.)

8. Border Crossings: Carlos Castaneda's Path of Knowledge.
Donald Lee Williams (Boulder). ISBN 0-919123-07-4. 160 pp. $12
The first thorough psychological examination of the Don Juan novels, bringing Castaneda's spiritual journey down to earth.

9. Narcissism and Character Transformation.
Nathan Schwartz-Salant (New York). ISBN 0-919123-08-2. 192 pp. $13
A comprehensive study of narcissism, drawing upon a variety of analytic points of view (Jung, Freud, Kohut, Klein, etc.). Illustrated.

10. Rape and Ritual: A Psychological Study.
Bradley A. Te Paske (Minneapolis). ISBN 0-919123-09-0. 160 pp. $12
An incisive combination of theory, clinical material and mythology, penetrating far beyond the actual deed to the archetypal background of sexual assault. Special attention to male ambivalence toward women. Illustrated.

11. Alcoholism and Women: The Background and the Psychology.
Jan Bauer (Montreal). ISBN 0-919123-10-4. 144 pp. $12
A major contribution to the subject, based on sociology, case material, dream analysis and archetypal patterns from mythology.

12. Addiction to Perfection: The Still Unravished Bride.
Marion Woodman (Toronto). ISBN 0-919123-11-2. 208 pp. $12
A powerful and authoritative look at the psychology and attitudes of modern women. Examines the feminine through dreams, mythology, food rituals, body imagery, sexuality and creativity. Illustrated.

13. Jungian Dream Interpretation: Theory and Practice.
James A. Hall, M.D. (Dallas). ISBN 0-919123-12-0. 128 pp. $12
A practical guide to an understanding of dreams, with many clinical examples. Particular attention to common dream motifs and compensation.

14. The Creation of Consciousness: Jung's Myth for Modern Man.
Edward F. Edinger (Los Angeles). ISBN 0-919123-13-9. 128 pp. $12
A new world-view based on Jung's life and work, proposing a creative collaboration between the scientific pursuit of knowledge and the religious search for meaning. Illustrated. (See also titles 22 and 24)

15. The Analytic Encounter: Transference and Relationship.
Mario Jacoby (Zurich). ISBN 0-919123-14-7. 128 pp. $12
A sensitive exploration of the difference between relationships based on projection and those characterized by objectivity and mutual respect.

16. Change of Life: Dreams and the Menopause.
Ann Mankowitz (Santa Fe). ISBN 0-919123-15-5. 128 pp. $12
A moving account of a menopausal woman's Jungian analysis, dramatically revealing the later years as a unique opportunity for psychological growth.

17. The Illness That We Are: A Jungian Critique of Christianity.
John P. Dourley (Ottawa). ISBN 0-919123-16-3. 128 pp. $12
A radical study exploring Jung's qualified appreciation of Christian symbols and ritual in light of mystical and alchemical traditions. (See title 7)

18. Hags and Heroes: Feminist Approach to Couple Psychotherapy.
Polly Young-Eisendrath (Philadelphia). ISBN 0-919123-17-1. 192 pp. $14
A highly original integration of feminist views with the concepts of Jung
and H.S. Sullivan. Detailed techniques, with emphasis on female authority.

19. Cultural Attitudes in Psychological Perspective.
Joseph Henderson (San Francisco). ISBN 0-919123-18-X. 128 pp. $12
A thoughtful new work by the co-author of *Man and His Symbols*, showing
how a psychological attitude can give depth and substance to social,
religious, aesthetic and philosophic attitudes. Illustrated.

20. The Vertical Labyrinth: Individuation in Jungian Psychology.
Aldo Carotenuto (Rome). ISBN 0-919123-19-8. 144 pp. $12
A guided journey through the world of dreams and psychic reality, showing
how the slow and often painful steps in individual psychological development parallel the historical evolution of consciousness. (See also title 25)

21. The Pregnant Virgin: Psychological Transformation.
Marion Woodman (Toronto). ISBN 0-919123-20-1. 208 pp. $15
A celebration of the feminine, in both men and women. Explores the search
for one's personal identity and unique potential, through the wisdom of the
body, eating disorders, relationships, dreams, addictions, etc. Illustrated.

22. Encounter with the Self: A Jungian Commentary on William Blake's *Illustrations of the Book of Job*.
Edward F. Edinger (Los Angeles). ISBN 0-919123-21-X. 80 pp. $10
A penetrating commentary on the Job story as an archetypal image of a
typical encounter between ego and Self. **Includes Blake's 22 drawings.**

23. The Scapegoat Complex: Shadow and Guilt.
Sylvia Brinton Perera (New York). ISBN 0-919123-22-8. 128 pp. $12
A hard-hitting study of scapegoat psychology as it manifests in modern
men and women, based on underlying archetypal patterns in mythology.

24. The Bible and the Psyche: Individuation in the Old Testament.
Edward F. Edinger (Los Angeles). ISBN 0-919123-23-6. 176 pp. $15
A major new work relating biblical events to the psychological movement
toward wholeness that takes place in modern men and women.

25. The Spiral Way: A Woman's Healing Journey.
Aldo Carotenuto (Rome). ISBN 0-919123-24-4. 144 pp. $13
A detailed case history of a 50-year-old woman's Jungian analysis, with
particular attention to her dreams and the rediscovery of her energy.

26. The Jungian Experience: Analysis and Individuation.
James A. Hall, M.D. (Dallas). ISBN 0-919123-25-2. 176 pp. $14
A comprehensive study of the clinical application of Jungian thought,
including details of the process of analysis, how and where to find an
analyst, location of training centers and recommended reading.

Add $1 per book (bookpost) or $3 per book (airmail)

INNER CITY BOOKS
Box 1271, Station Q, Toronto, Canada M4T 2P4   (416) 927-0355

ORDER FORM
Please detach and fill out both sides

Prices quoted are in $U.S. (except for Cdn. orders)

POSTAGE/HANDLING
Add $1 per book (bookpost) or $3 per book (airmail)

Title	Price	Copies	Amount
1. Raven	$10	_____	_____
2. Redemption	$10	_____	_____
3. Divination	$10	_____	_____
4. The Owl	$10	_____	_____
5. Alchemy	$16	_____	_____
6. Descent	$10	_____	_____
7. Psyche	$10	_____	_____
8. Border	$12	_____	_____
9. Narcissism	$13	_____	_____
10. Rape	$12	_____	_____
11. Alcoholism	$12	_____	_____
12. Addiction	$12	_____	_____
13. Dream	$12	_____	_____
14. Creation	$12	_____	_____
15. Encounter	$12	_____	_____
16. Change	$12	_____	_____
17. Illness	$12	_____	_____
18. Hags	$14	_____	_____
19. Culture	$12	_____	_____
20. Labyrinth	$12	_____	_____
21. Virgin	$15	_____	_____
22. Self	$10	_____	_____
23. Scapegoat	$12	_____	_____
24. Bible	$15	_____	_____
25. Spiral	$13	_____	_____
26. Experience	$14	_____	_____

Subtotal: _____

Plus Postage/Handling: _____

TOTAL: _____

Orders from outside Canada pay in $U.S.

Please make check or money order (no credit cards)
payable to INNER CITY BOOKS

INNER CITY BOOKS
Box 1271, Station Q
Toronto, Canada M4T 2P4

Check or Money Order enclosed for ———

Please send books to:

NAME: ——————————————

ADDRESS: ——————————————

——————————— Zip or Postal Code: ———

Please send ——— (quantity) Catalogues/Order Forms to me ——— and ——— to:

NAME: ——————————————

ADDRESS: ——————————————

——————————— Zip or Postal Code: ———

REMARKS